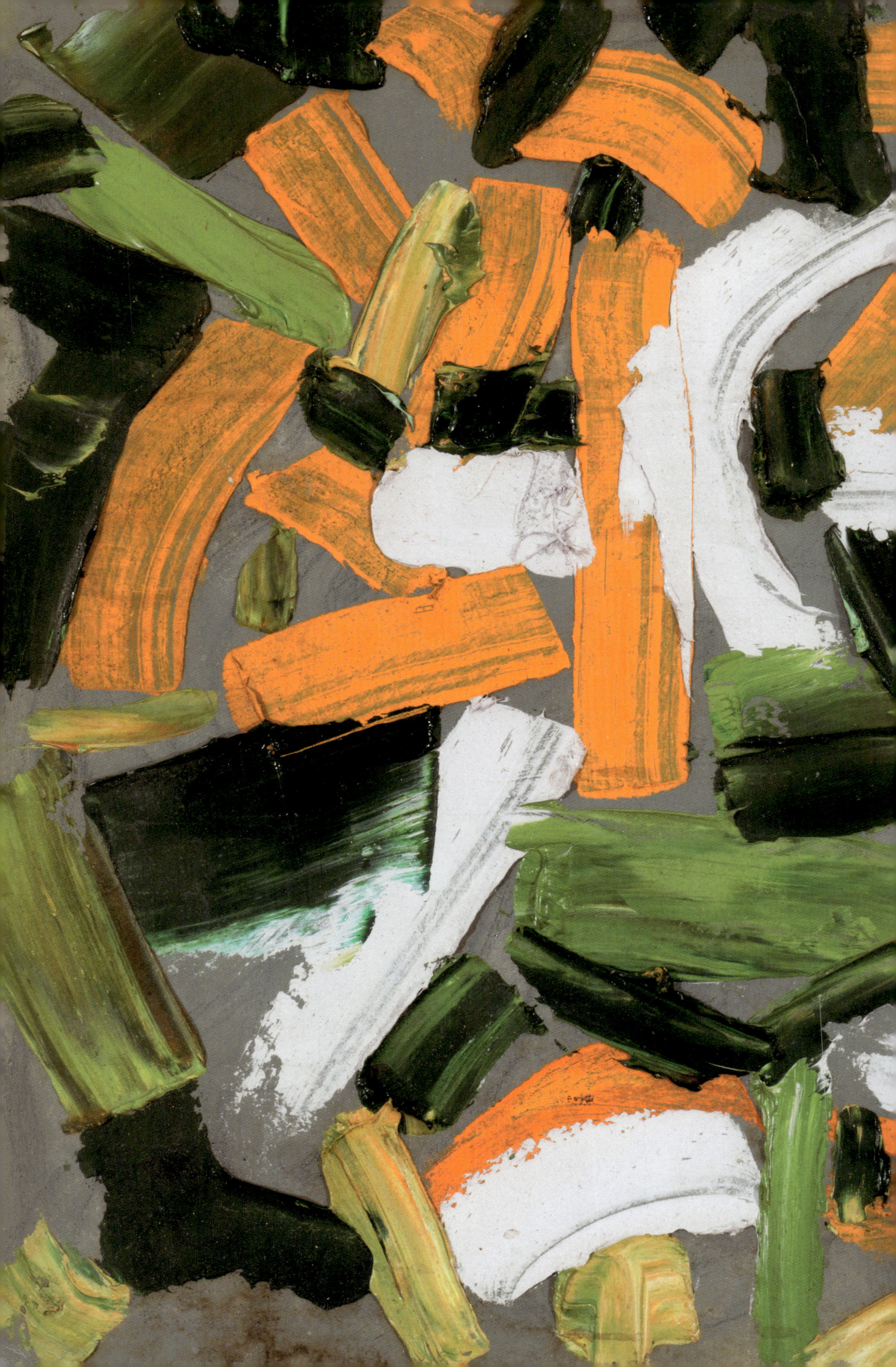

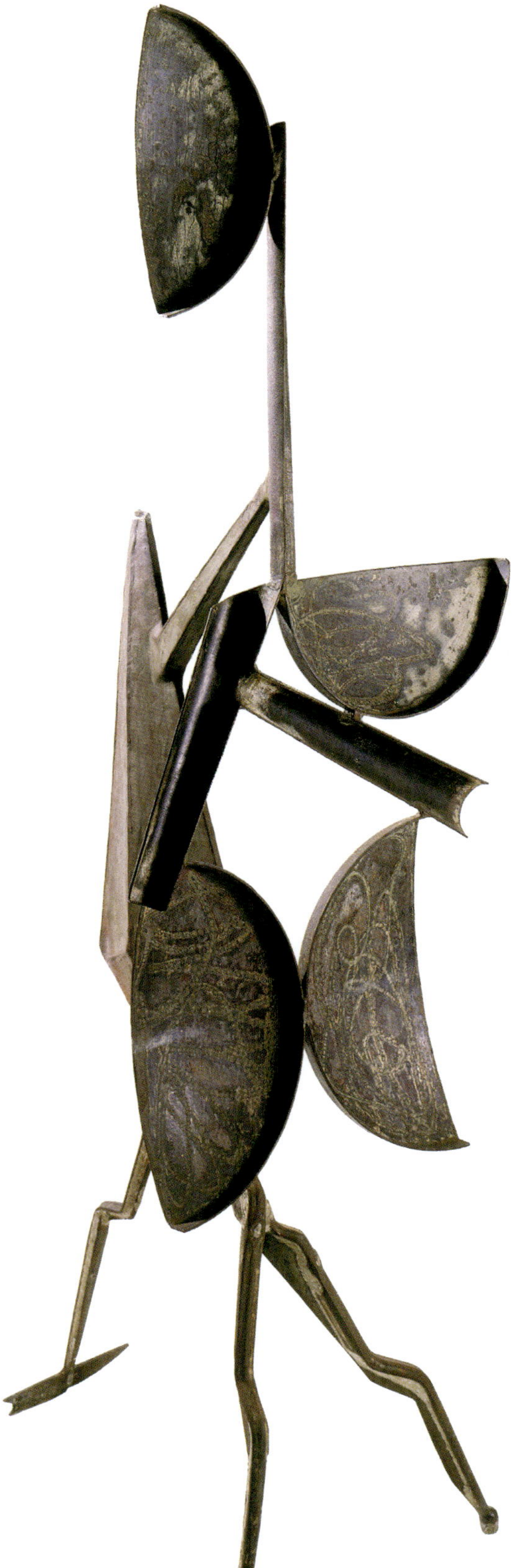

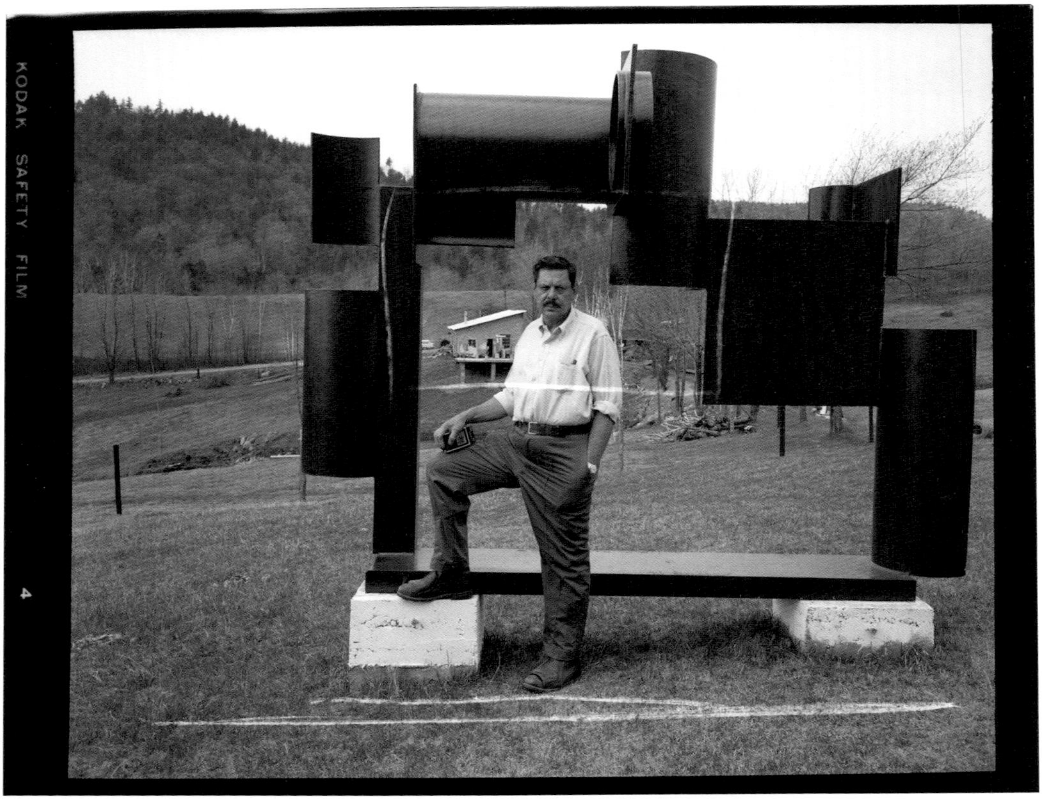
KODAK SAFETY FILM
4

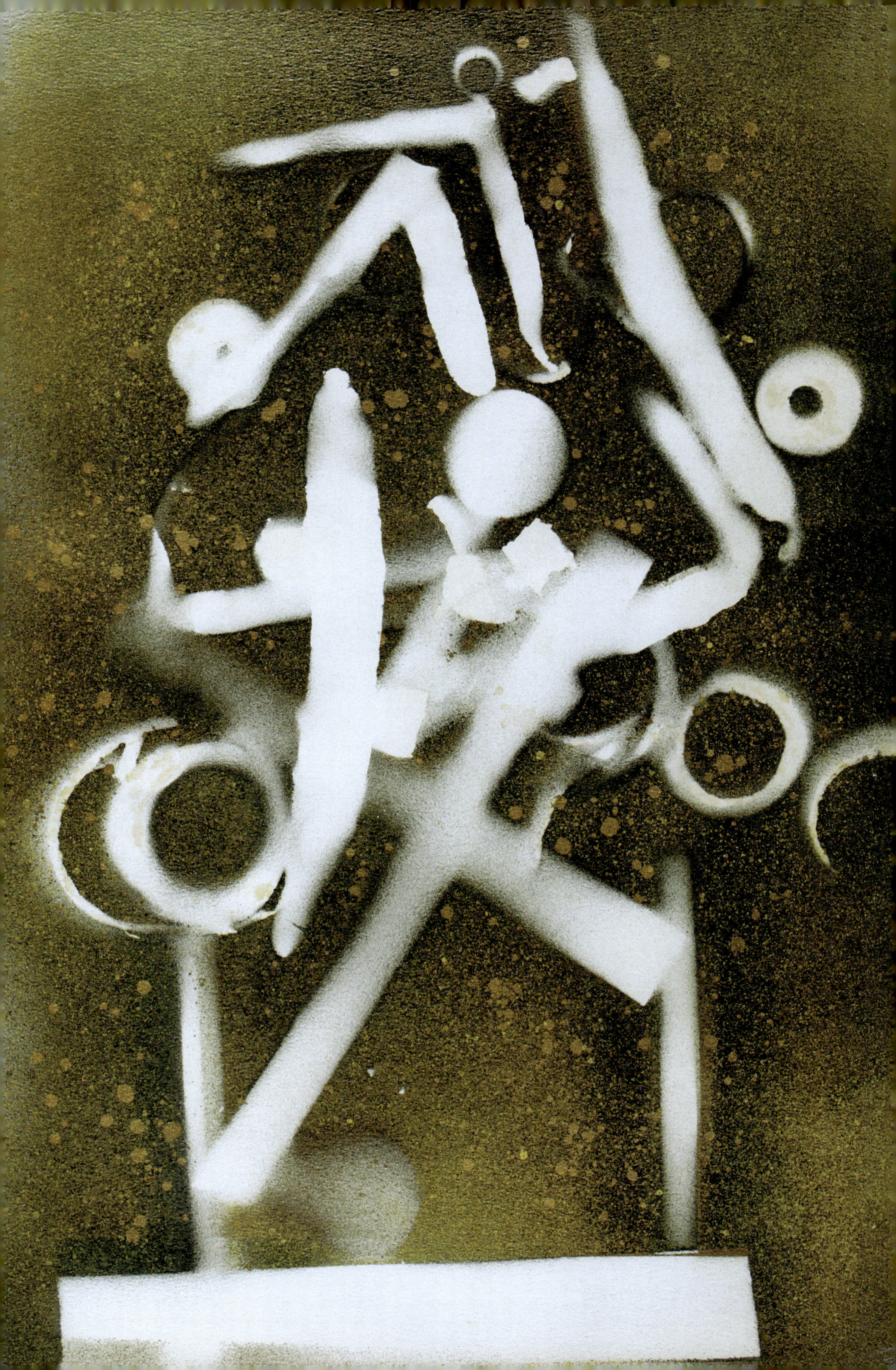

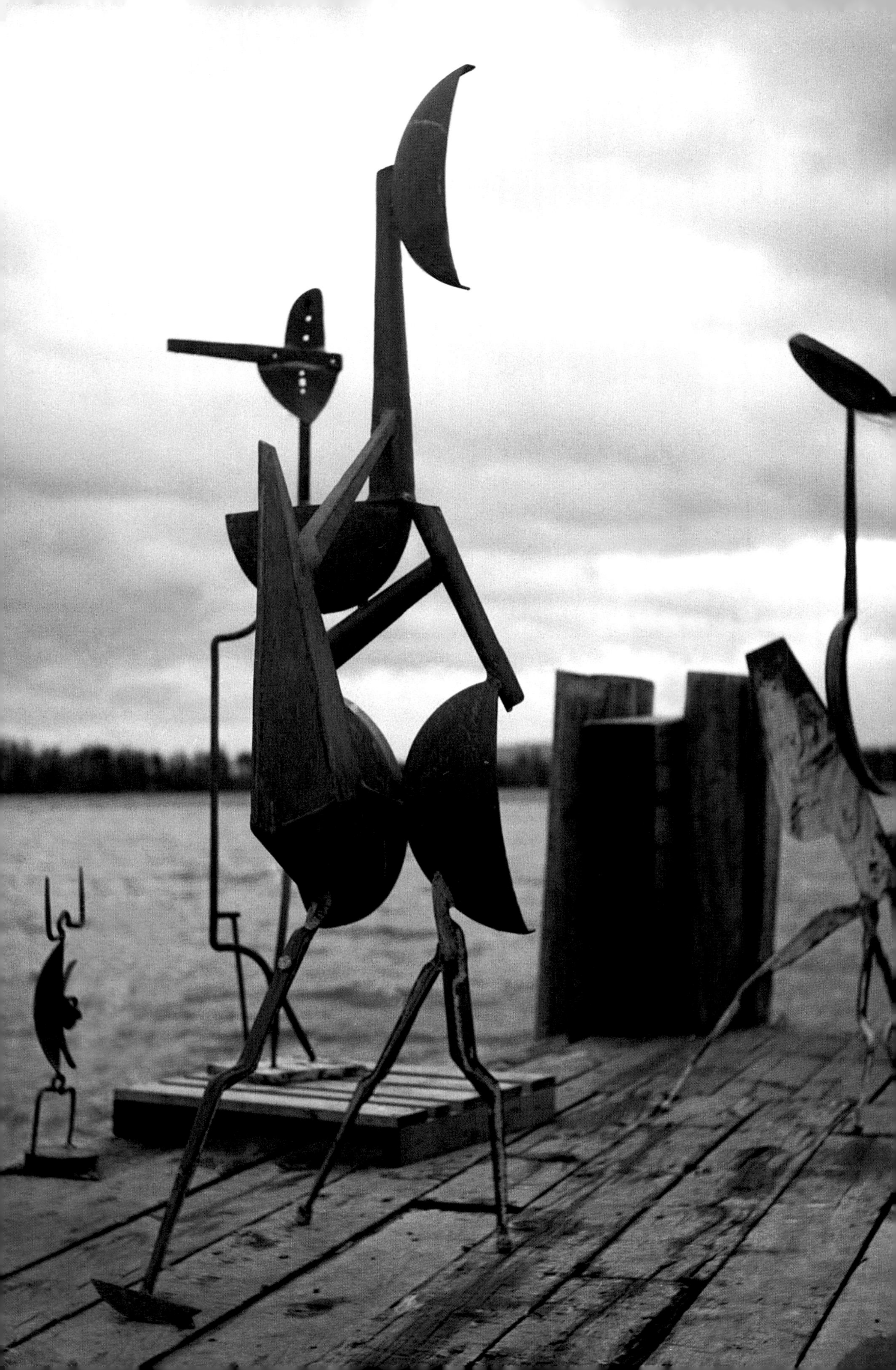

DAVID SMITH INVENTS

SUSAN BEHRENDS FRANK

With essays by Sarah Hamill and Peter Stevens

The Phillips Collection in association with Yale University Press, New Haven and London

CONTENTS

FOREWORD

David Smith Invents draws its inspiration from two recent gifts to The Phillips Collection – its first sculpture and work on paper by this major American artist, whose reputation has grown steadily since his death in 1965. These newly acquired works – an important sculpture, *Bouquet of Concaves*, and a gestural, black egg ink drawing – date from 1959, when Smith was engaged in making a sustained series of calligraphic brush and ink drawings and shifting his sculptural emphasis to upright, geometric, relief-like abstractions.

The acquisition of significant works by one of the giants of American art creates an occasion to expand our understanding of the artist. Although the Phillips has only recently been able to claim Smith as one of its artists, its founder, Duncan Phillips, recognized him as deserving a place in the Collection and made sure that the museum was a venue in 1962 for the Museum of Modern Art's superb Smith retrospective featuring some fifty sculptures. Our project, *David Smith Invents*, is the twenty-first century manifestation of that institutional recognition. To understand Smith's commanding aesthetic vision and his contributions to modernism in the second half of the twentieth century, one must understand his approach to his materials, his use of color, and the interplay between his sculpture, paintings, drawings, and photographs. With its focus on a closely related group of works in all media from the early 1950s to the early 1960s, *David Smith Invents* gives fresh insight into the aesthetic concerns of this celebrated artist during his last decade. Organized by The Phillips Collection, this is the first exhibition devoted to David Smith in Washington, D.C., in nearly thirty years.

Putting together the exhibition and this publication required the collaboration of many people. The Phillips Collection is deeply indebted to the Estate of David Smith for its support of this project from initial curatorial proposal to its realization in the galleries and accompanying book. Peter Stevens, executive director of the Estate, has shared with us his insights about Smith, beginning with his thoughtful assessment of the *Bouquet of Concaves* in our conservation studio more than two years ago. The Estate has provided access to its archival materials and loaned nineteen works to the exhibition.

At the Phillips I would like to express my deepest gratitude to Susan Behrends Frank, PhD, associate curator for research, who proposed this project, shaped it, wrote the lead essay for the book, and oversaw every detail of the exhibition and publication. A special word of thanks is due to Johanna Halford-MacLeod, editor in chief, who worked tirelessly to create a beautiful publication.

Dorothy Kosinski, PhD
Director, The Phillips Collection

"The poetic vision in sculpture is fully as free as in painting. Like a painting, sculpture now deals in the illusion of form as well as its own particular property of form itself."

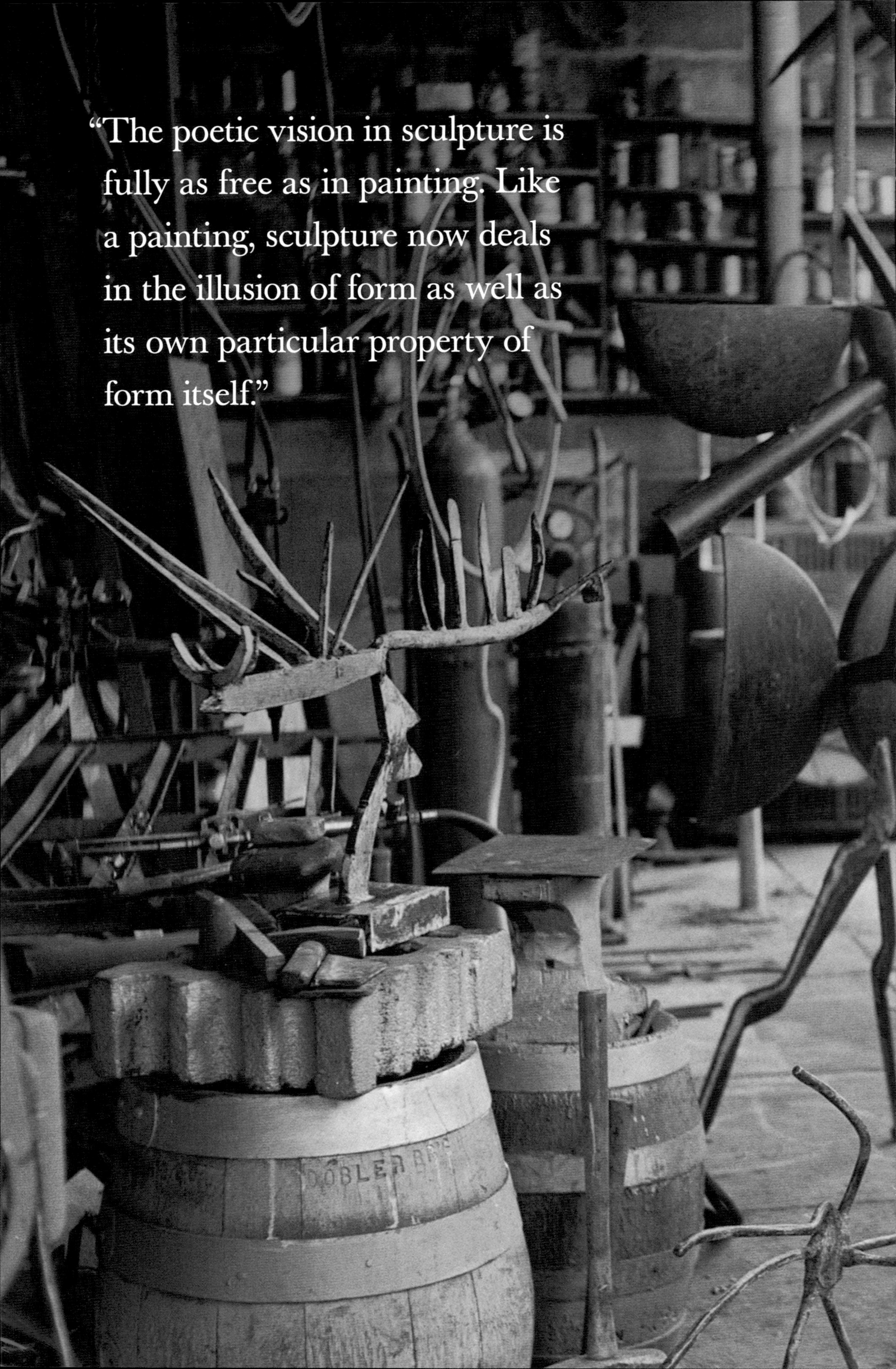

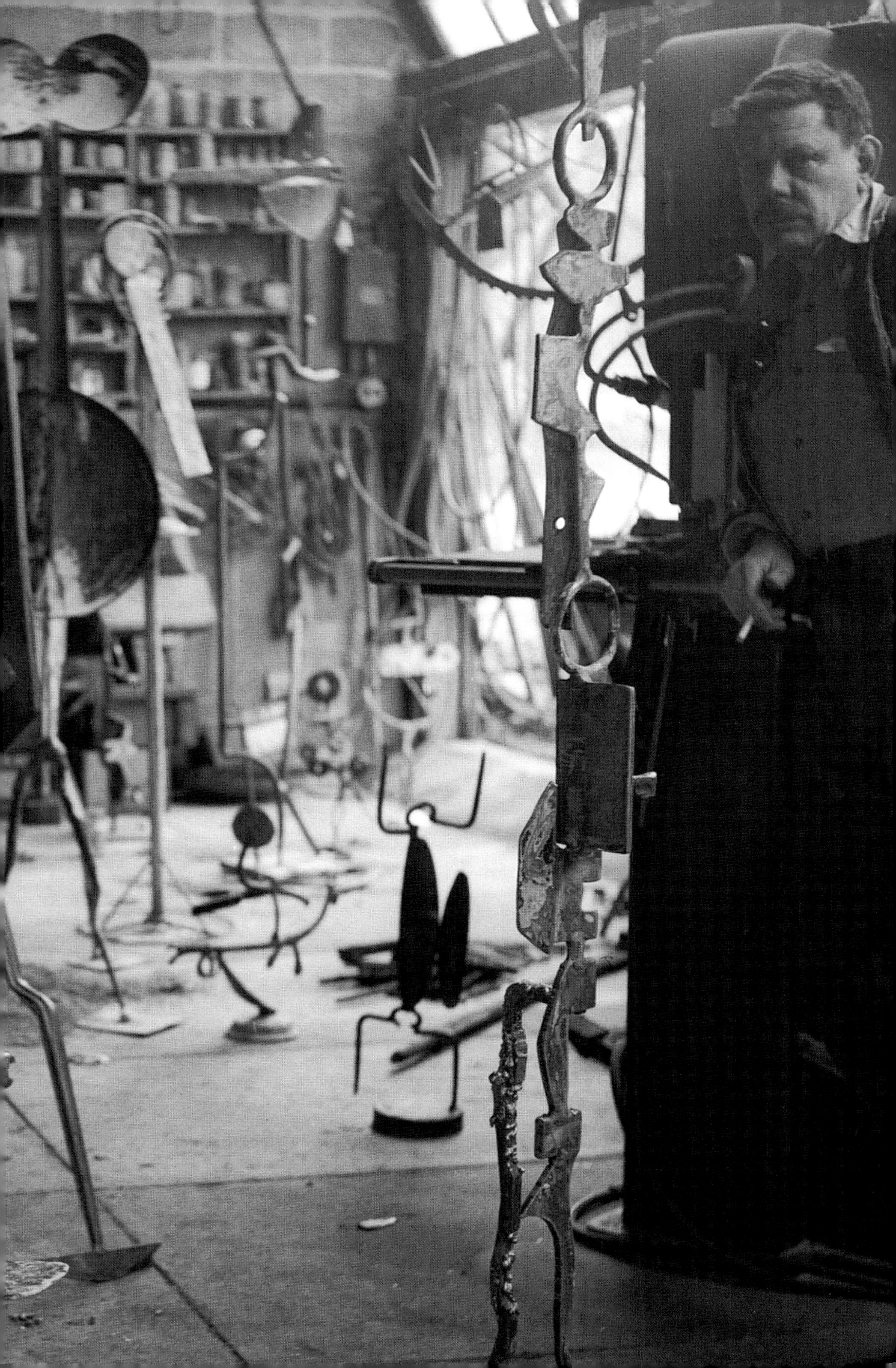

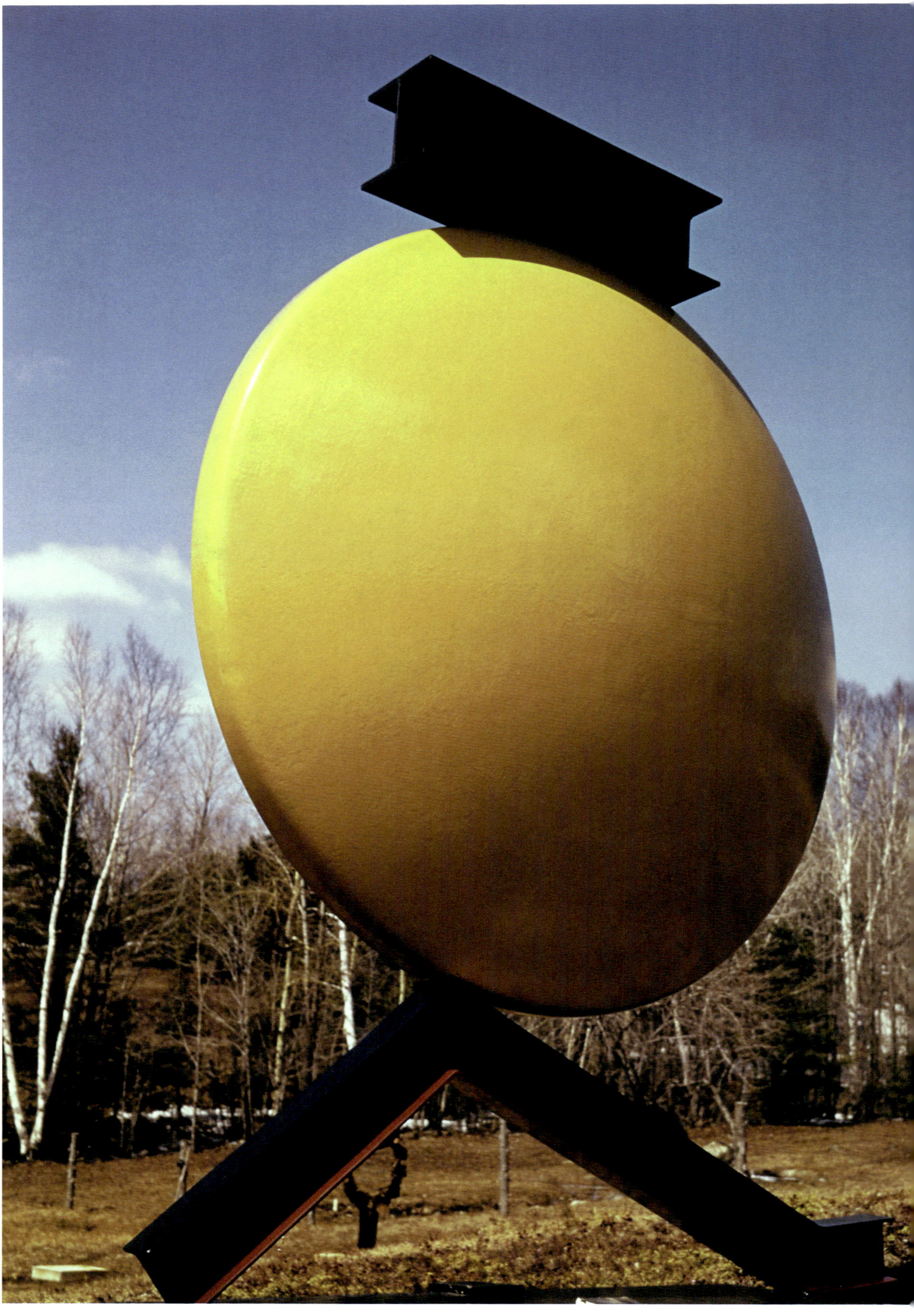

DAVID SMITH INVENTS

Susan Behrends Frank

In February 1960, *Arts* magazine published a "Special David Smith Number." Smith (1906–65), then in his mid-fifties, was already recognized by artists and critics at the time as the most important sculptor of the postwar years. Today he is considered one of the giants of American art and a pioneer in gaining for sculpture the respect previously reserved for painting in America.[1]

***Bec-Dida Day*, 1963, photograph by David Smith, c. 1963**

PREVIOUS: Self-portrait in the workshop at Bolton Landing, 1953

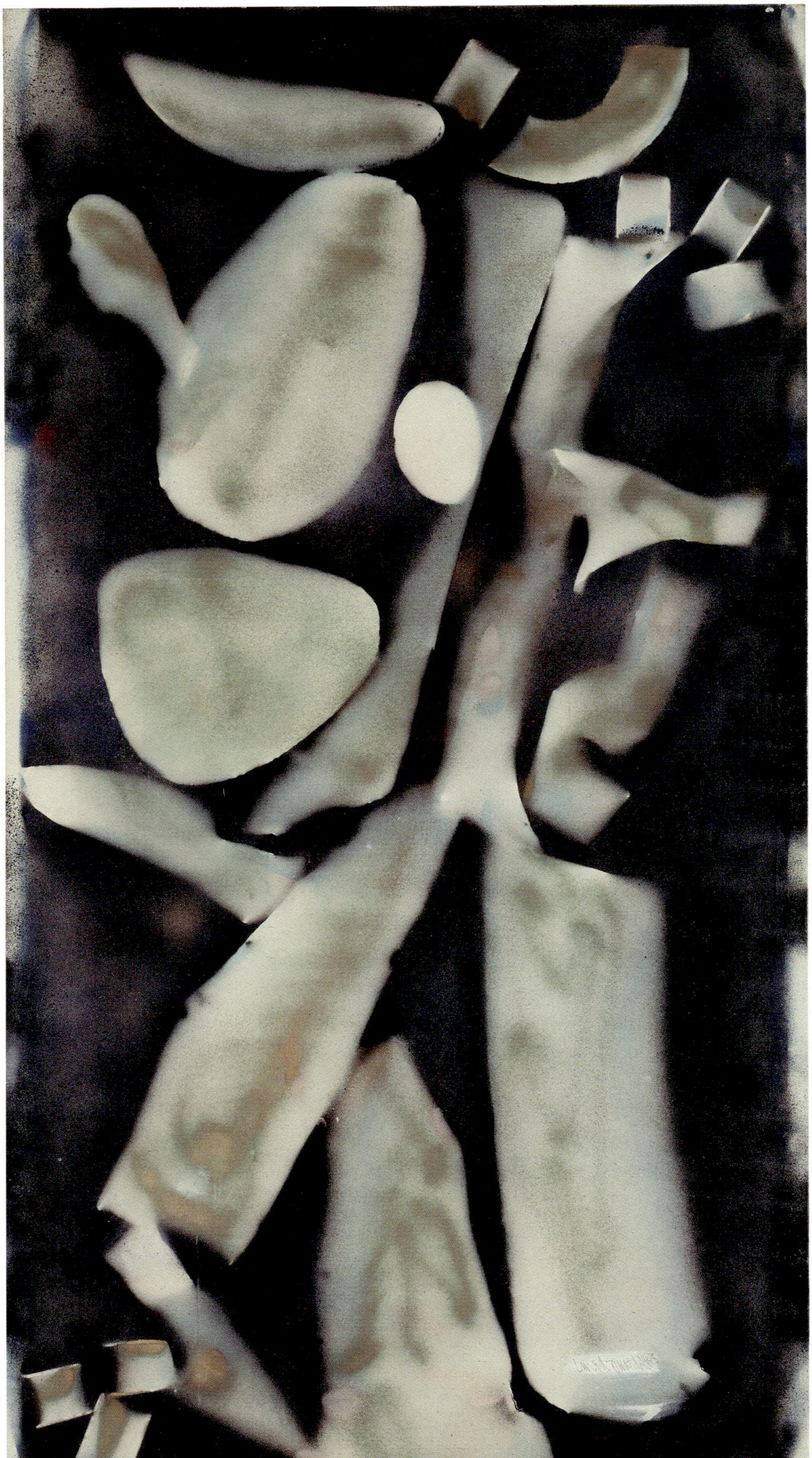

For the *Arts* issue, Smith collaborated for months with his friend, the magazine's editor, Hilton Kramer.[2] Their intent was to provide a dynamic statement about Smith's current work along with a thoughtful retrospective of his oeuvre in all media. By the end of the 1950s, Smith was poised to begin the abstract and monumental works that would seal

"I don't know whether I make some pieces as painted sculpture or paintings in form."

his reputation as a modern master. With a major retrospective at the Museum of Modern Art in 1957 and participation in both the twenty-ninth Venice Biennale (1958) and the fifth São Paolo Bienal (1959), Smith was already enjoying international and critical success, when *Arts* anointed him by making him its first featured cover artist.

Trained at the Art Students League in New York (1927–31), Smith identified himself as a painter who came to sculpture through cubism and montage, becoming, in 1933, the first American to make welded steel sculpture.[3] Dissolving the boundaries between two- and three-dimensional work and merging the concerns of painting and sculpture was a primary aspect of Smith's aesthetic. Although he expressed himself primarily through welded steel constructions, Smith never stopped drawing or painting. He identified himself as a painter-sculptor in the modern tradition and believed the breadth of his imaginings required him to work in a variety of media, whether in two or three dimensions.

***White Egg with Pink*, 1958, oil and metallic paint on canvas**

The fluidity with which his ideas passed between media permitted him to break the rules defining sculptural form and to challenge perception by exploring the interplay between pictorial illusionism as two-dimensional surface and as three-dimensional construction. He often stated that he never recognized "any separation" between painting and sculpture "except in one element of dimension."[4] Working pictorially and two-dimensionally was second nature to him, and the surface of his sculptures was always his to control and define. About his work, he conceded: "I don't know whether I make some pieces as painted sculpture or paintings in form."[5]

Smith was at heart a poet and a romantic who took his inspiration from the natural world, as well as from literature, philosophy, music, and art. A Midwesterner, he learned to weld as a college student one summer at a Studebaker automobile plant in Indiana before making his way to New York. He attributed his mental "liberation" to an extended trip to England, France, Greece, and Russia, in 1935–36, but knew that he belonged in and to America: "The one thing when I came back that I realized was that I belonged here; my materials were here, my thoughts were here, my birth was here, and whatever I could do had to be done here."[6] In 1940 he moved permanently to a farm near Lake George in upstate New York, some 200 miles north of New York City. There, at Bolton Landing, surrounded by the Adirondacks, he pursued painting and sculpture as the same enterprise with an all-consuming passion and focus. Whether in two or three dimensions, his art poured out of him in a steady stream that was at once spontaneous and intuitive, but also grounded in tradition,

***Untitled,* 1958, spray enamel on canvas**

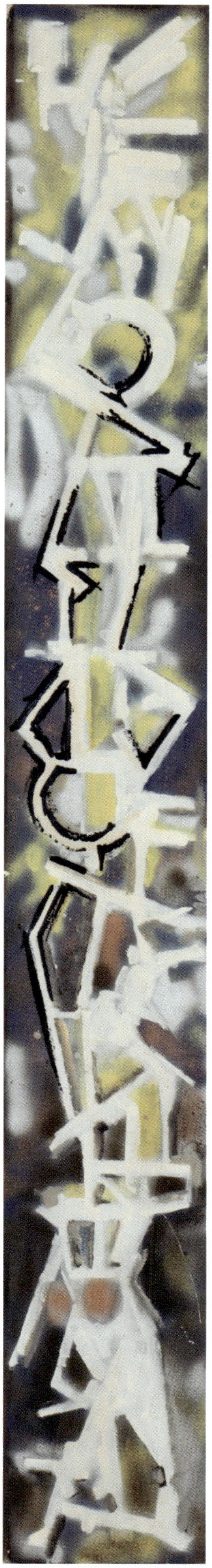

informed by his wide-ranging intellect, acute visual memory, and vast knowledge of art throughout history, including that of his own time.

By the mid-1950s Smith's sculptural process was intuitive and improvisational. Rather than sketching out an idea and buying the material for it, Smith worked directly and spontaneously, discovering in the sorting and touching of the hard steel those elements that would "fit a niche in my mind, fit into a relationship I need."[7] He shared with the cubists and the abstract artists of the postwar period the belief that the materials themselves, and his response to them, dictated the direction to follow in the work. Rarely concerned with what he called "the Grand Conception," Smith had, as he wrote for the *Arts* article, a "preoccupation with parts," their "unities and associations."[8] Working with steel tubing, boiler tank ends, angle irons, and other industrial parts ordered from catalogues, as well as with steel obtained as waste, Smith incorporated into his process what he described as "perceptual curing," the daily study of the hard steel strewn outside the workshop before choosing elements and deciding how to arrange them into a final whole. As he expressed it: "I cannot conceive a work and buy material for it. I can find or discover a part. To buy new material – I need a truckload before I can work on one. To look at it every day – to let it soften – to let it break up in segments, planes, lines, etc. – wrap itself in hazy shapes.... With possession and acquaintance, a fluidity develops which was not there the day it was unloaded...."[9]

Smith's increasingly ambitious metal improvisations in the 1950s used larger and heavier steel parts, which, because of their weight, required him

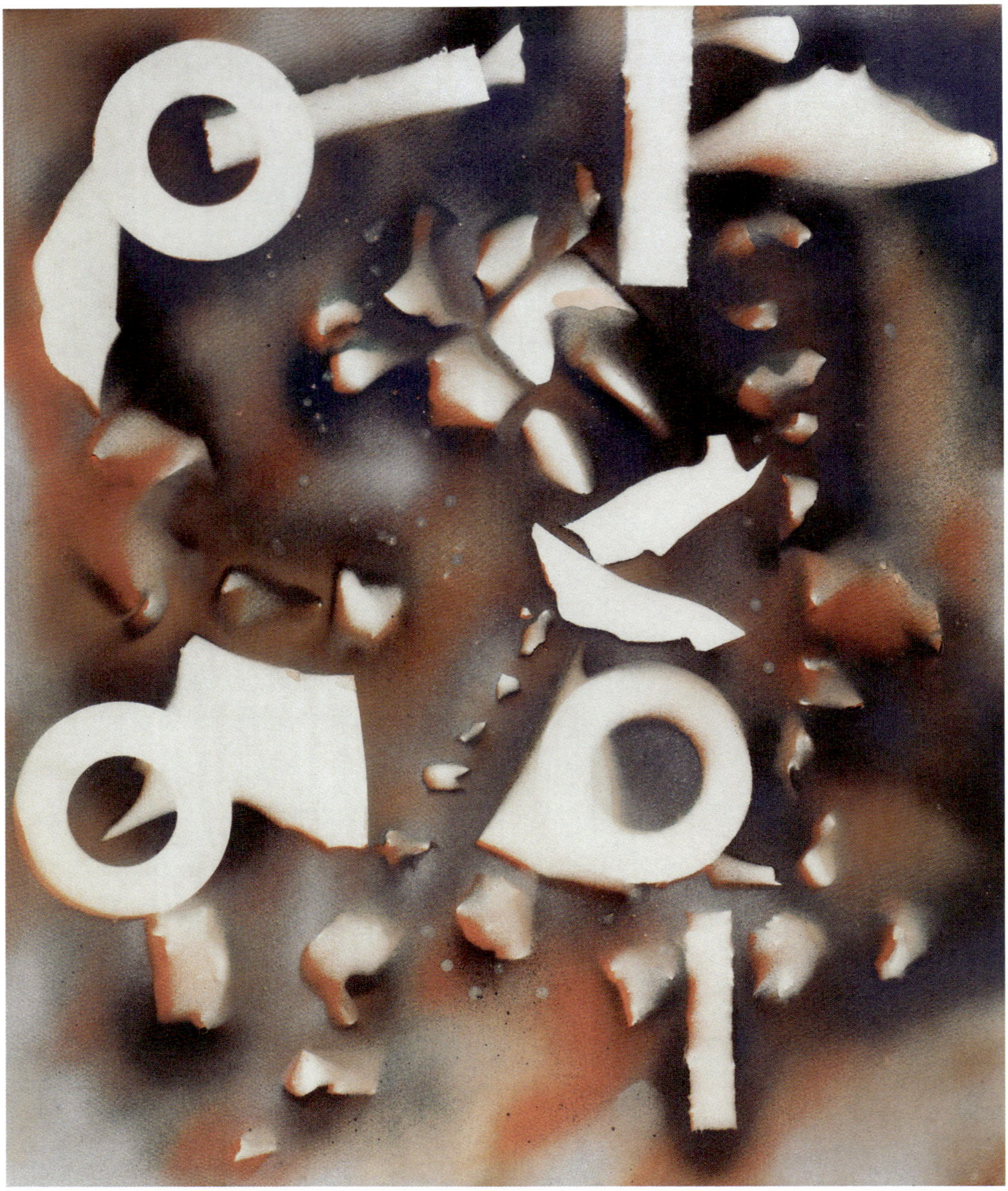

to work flat on the floor in a pictorial manner reminiscent of painter colleagues who had abandoned their easels for the studio floor (*page 79*). Annotating a photograph in the *Arts* issue, Smith wrote: "I paint white areas on the floor; lay out parts for relationships."[10] His inscription on his photograph of *Bouquet of Concaves* (1959) (*page 31*) reads: "Started out like many others on white steel palettes outside the shop – order and reorder – daily or at least looking until the parts cured into the whole."[11] As his photographs and annotations reveal, the white steel palettes and white rectangles painted on the floor functioned like drawing paper or canvas, mimicking a flat pictorial field on which he intuitively arranged steel parts as abstract forms before welding them together and uprighting the assemblage in order to complete it. In a 1964 interview,

"I paint white areas on the floor; lay out parts for relationships."

Thomas Hess, then editor of *Art News*, described Smith's welded steel sculptures as "drawings pulled up," which the artist agreed was appropriate.[12]

Smith thought of himself as an artist who combined industrial experiences, materials, and techniques into a personal expressive vision.[13] As part of the "new sculpture," Smith championed "the machine tool" as "an instrument of aesthetics...."[14] A disk grinder could be used, for example, as a tool to remove rust and clean the surface of the boiler tank ends before he incorporated them into sculptures. Leaving those burnished patterns visible, as in *Tanktotems III* and *IV* (*page 25*), transformed the hard steel into a pictorial surface embedded with Smith's gestural markings. His insight that the machinist's tool could be used on steel like an artist's brush or pen, culminated in the burnished reflective surfaces of his stainless steel works (*page 39*). As he proclaimed in 1951: "The change of one machine or tool to the other means no more than changing brushes to a painter or chisels to a carver."[15]

***Untitled*, c. 1959, spray enamel on canvas**

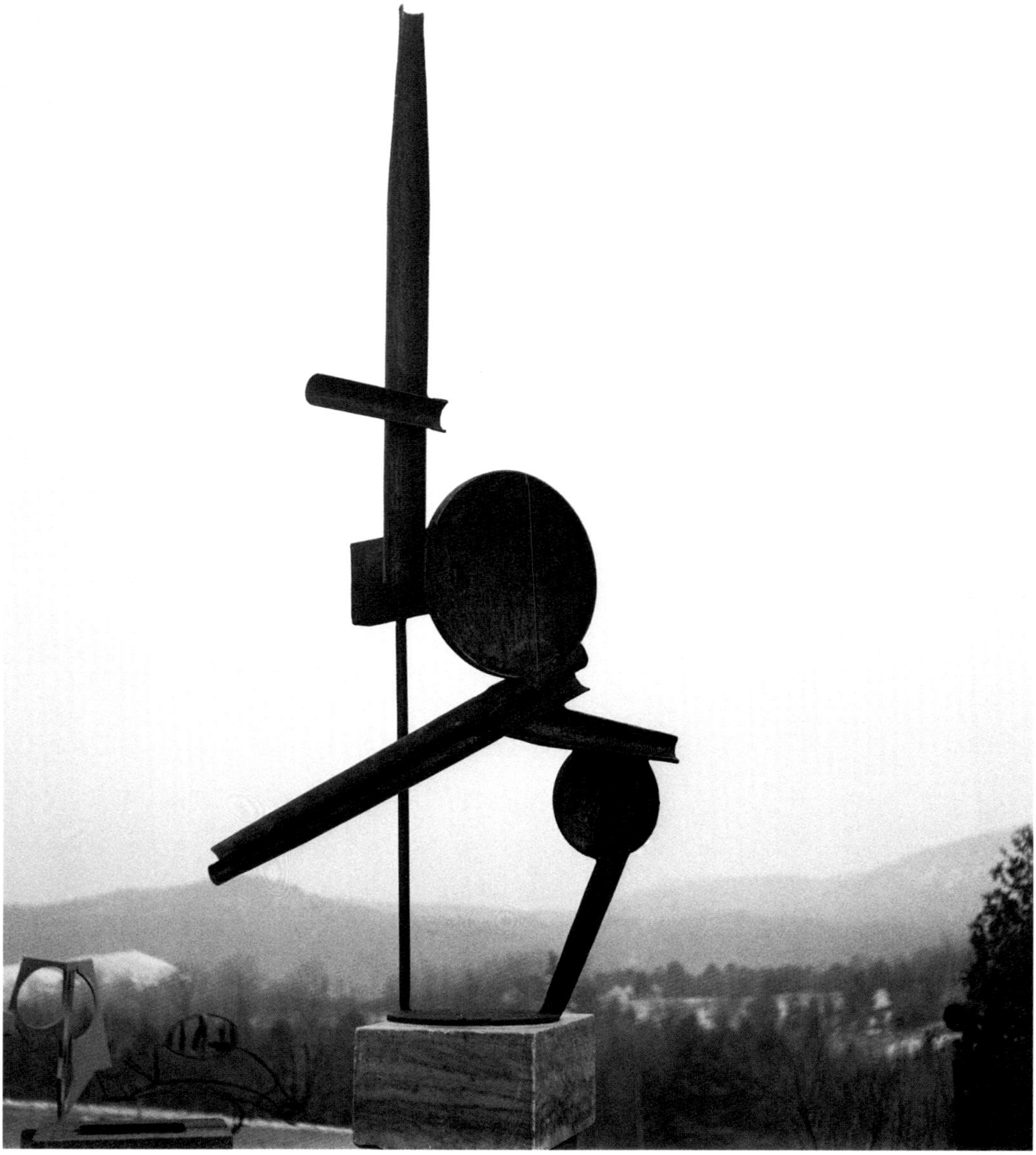

Tanktotem V,
1955–56, photograph
by David Smith

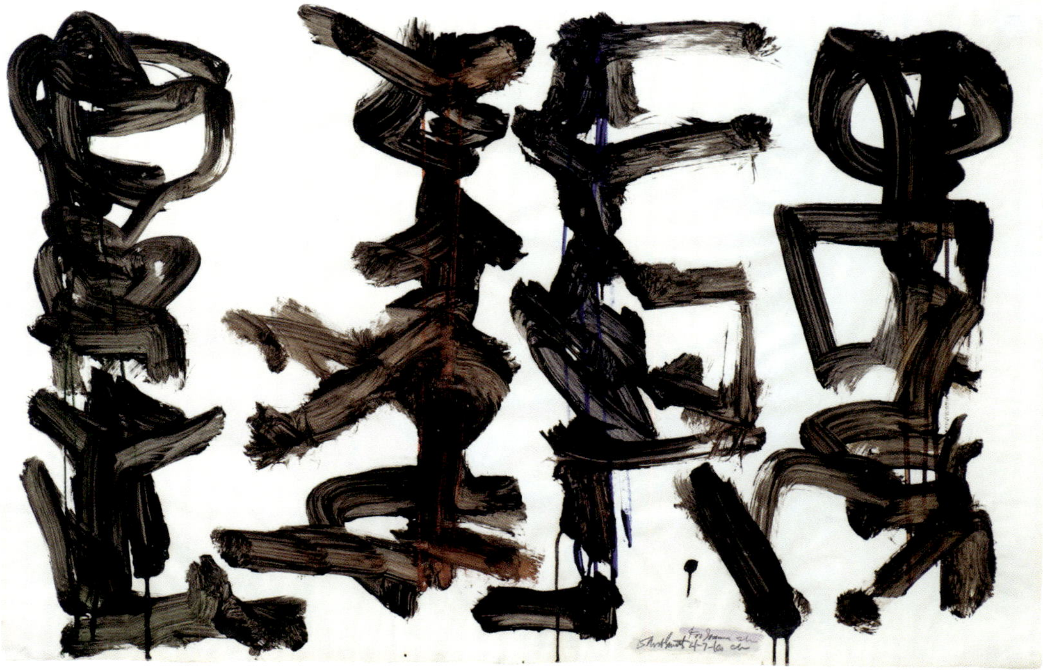

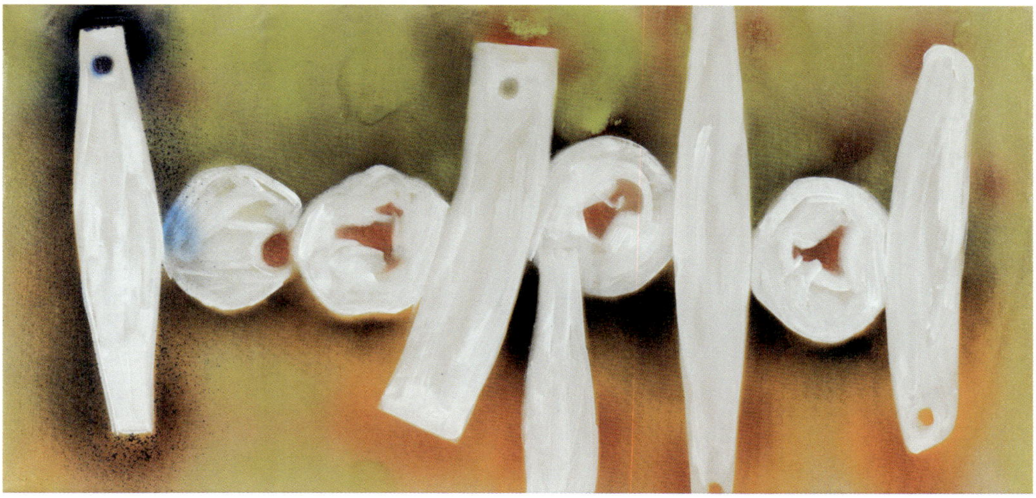

ABOVE: *Untitled*, 1960, egg ink and tempera on paper

BELOW: *Untitled*, 1964, spray enamel on canvas

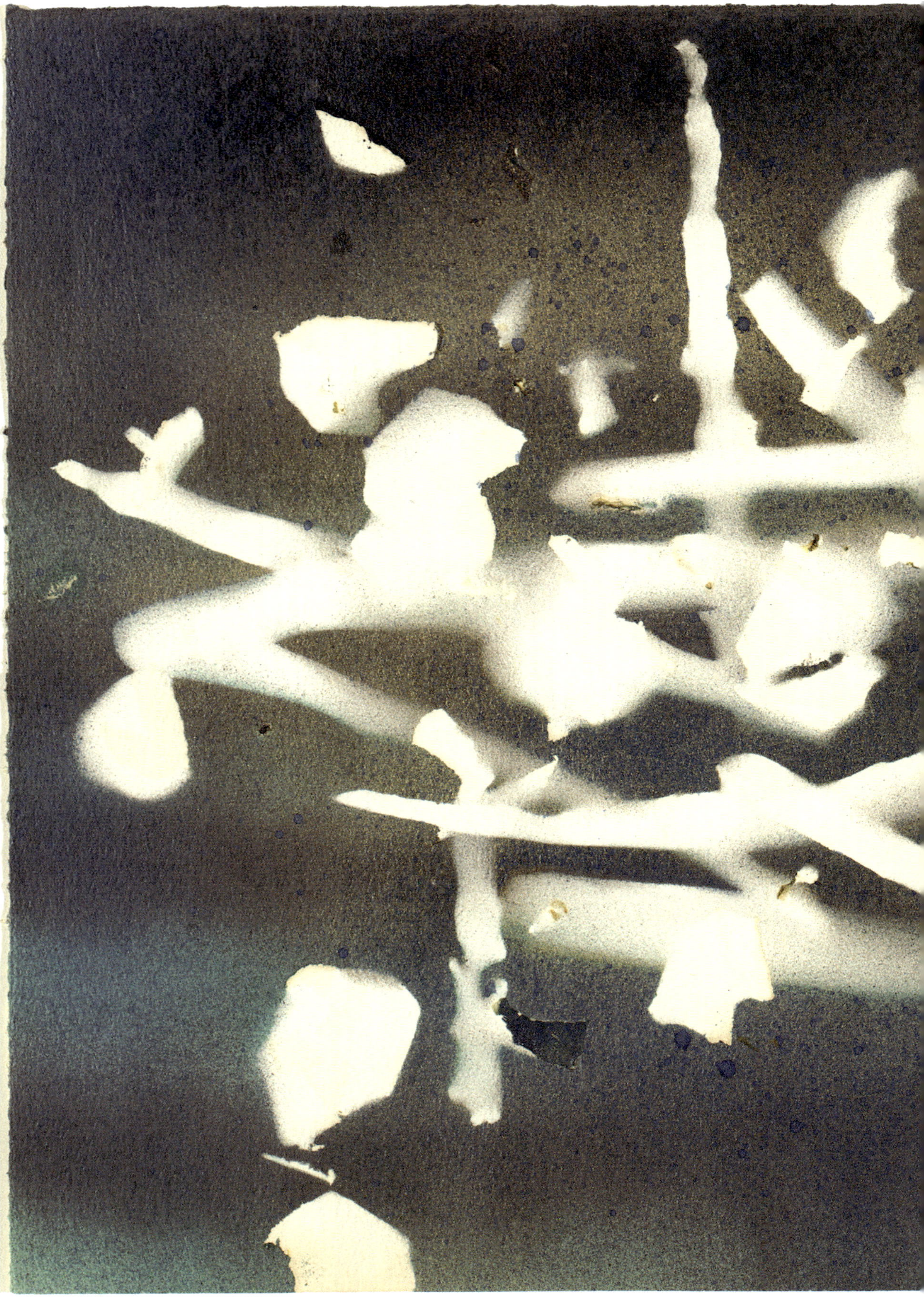

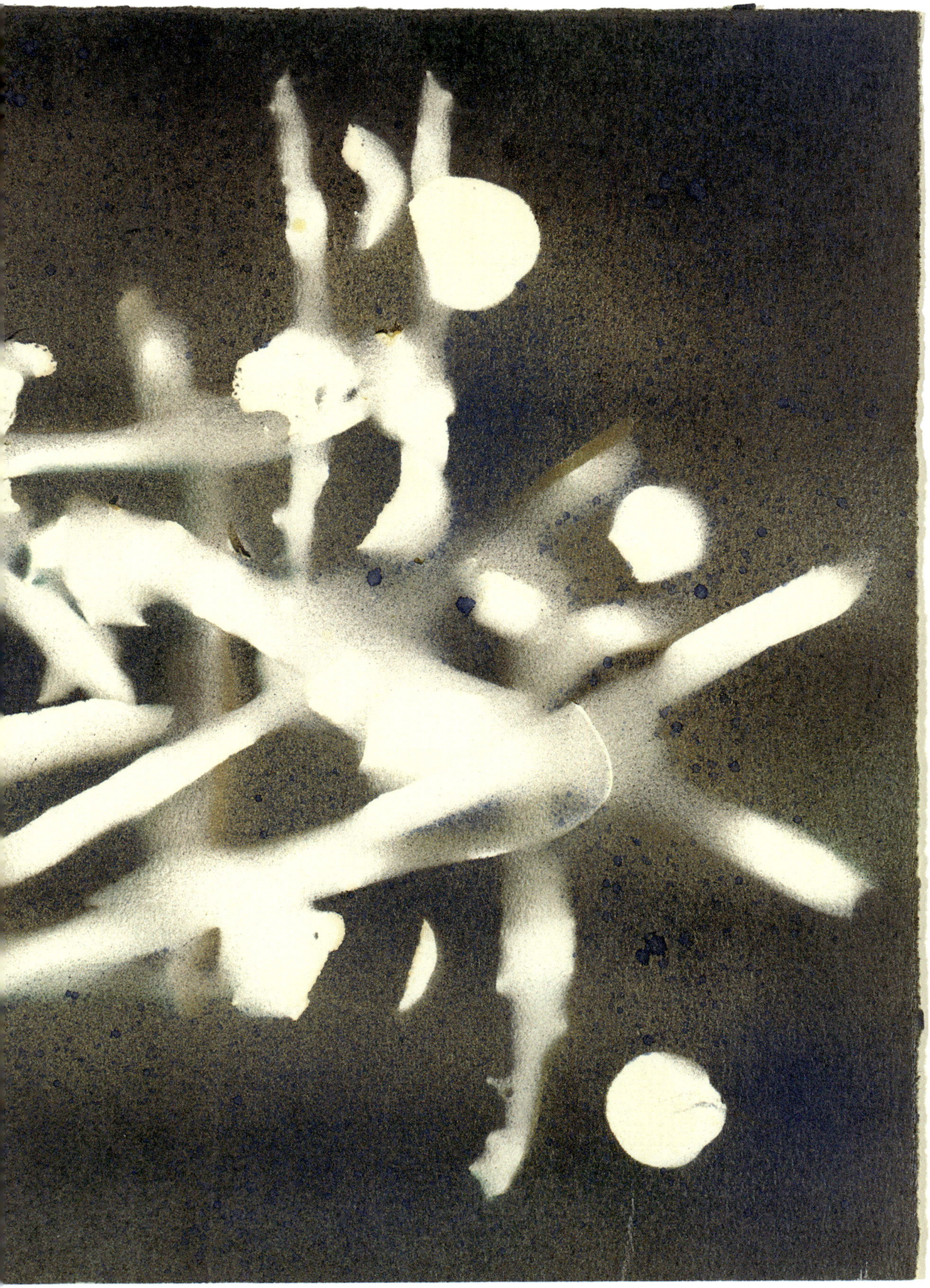

Always open to new directions and technical innovations related to his materials, Smith was influenced in his painting style by his own welding process. When commercial aerosol spray enamel first became available, he quickly added it to his arsenal of materials and, in 1957, started a new body of work on canvas and paper that combined his sculptural technique with stenciling.[16] These works were directly inspired by the silhouettes of negative form left by the dark "spray" of the arc welding process, revealed when Smith raised his sculptures into an upright position. Collectively known as Sprays, a reference to the paint material and the welding technique that inspired them, they feature negative forms and delicately colored atmospheres in canvases as high as eleven feet and works on paper as small as thirteen by ten inches. Some, like *White Egg with Pink* (1958), suggest that the voids are volumetric; others are flat abstract shapes or cosmic explosions suspended in layered mist (*page 14*). As Peter Stevens, executive director of the David Smith Estate, has explained: "The Sprays allowed Smith to manipulate three-dimensional objects, create two-dimensional picture planes, and transfer manifest gestures from hand to surface."[17] Although Smith's new paintings contradicted the expected emphasis in the 1950s on brushstroke as the personal mark of the painter, they continue his commitment to exploiting the interplay between the image and the object, which is central to his work.

A solo exhibition of Smith's paintings in September 1959 at French and Company, New York's newest salon of modernism, directed by Clement Greenberg, was the first major show dedicated to Smith's paintings, as well as the public unveiling of

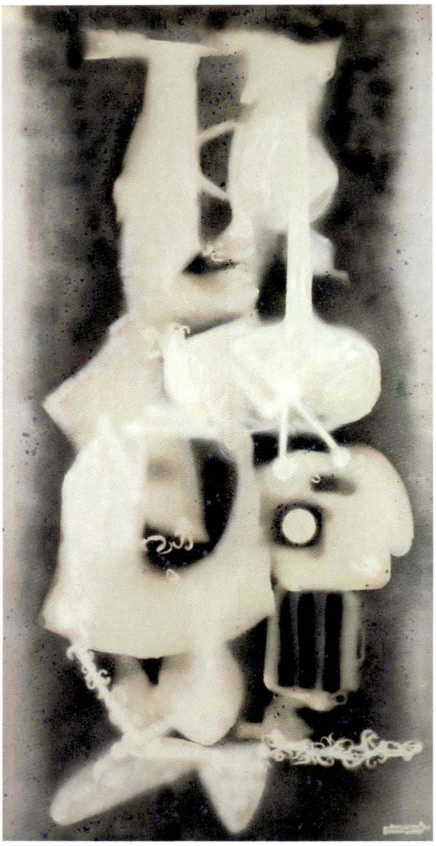

PREVIOUS: ***Untitled*, 1962, enamel spray paint on wove paper**

ABOVE: ***Untitled*, 1959, spray enamel on canvas**

RIGHT: ***Tanktotem IV*, 1953, photograph by David Smith**

NEXT: Sprays in the studio at Bolton Landing, c. 1959–60, photograph by David Smith

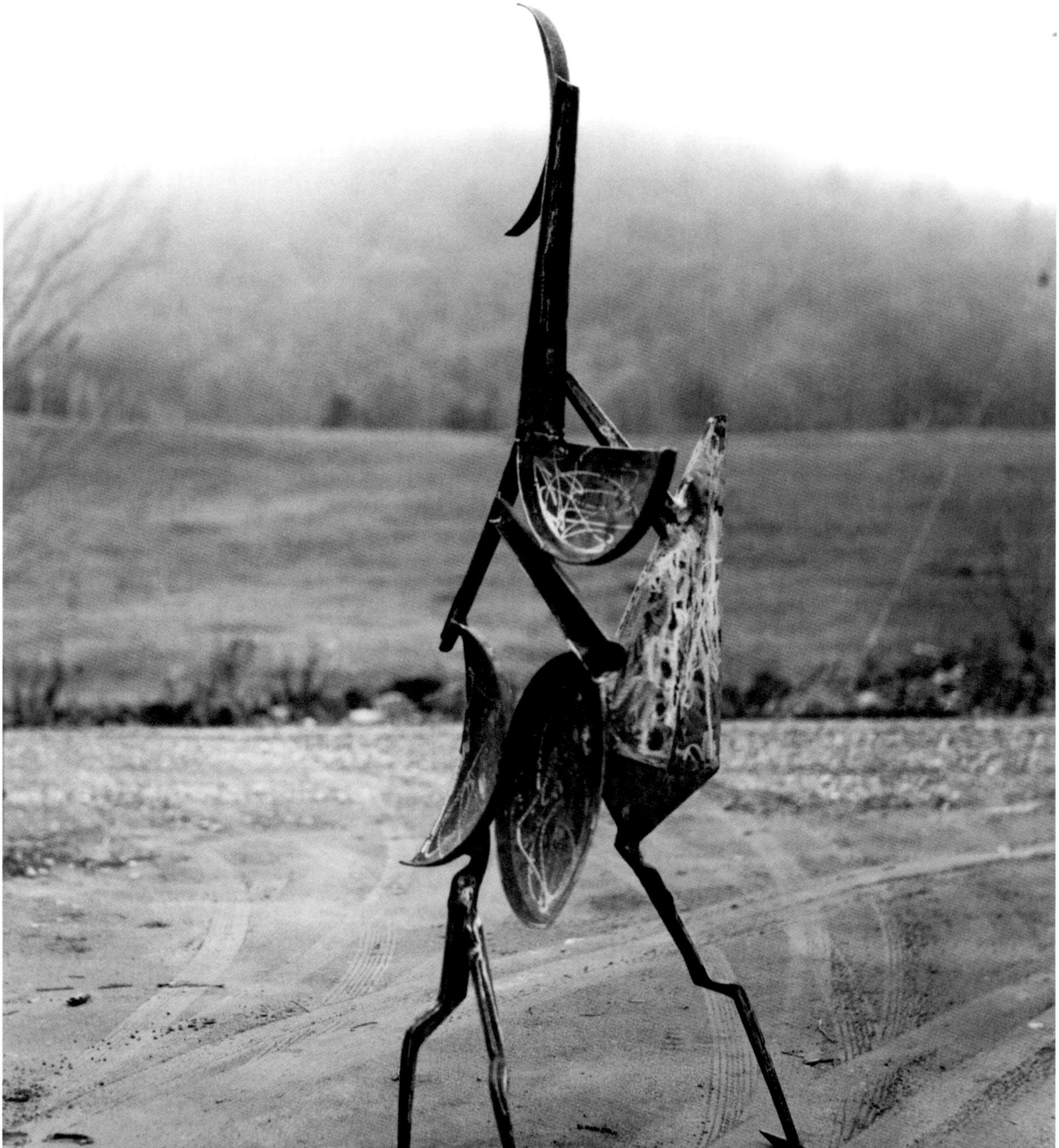

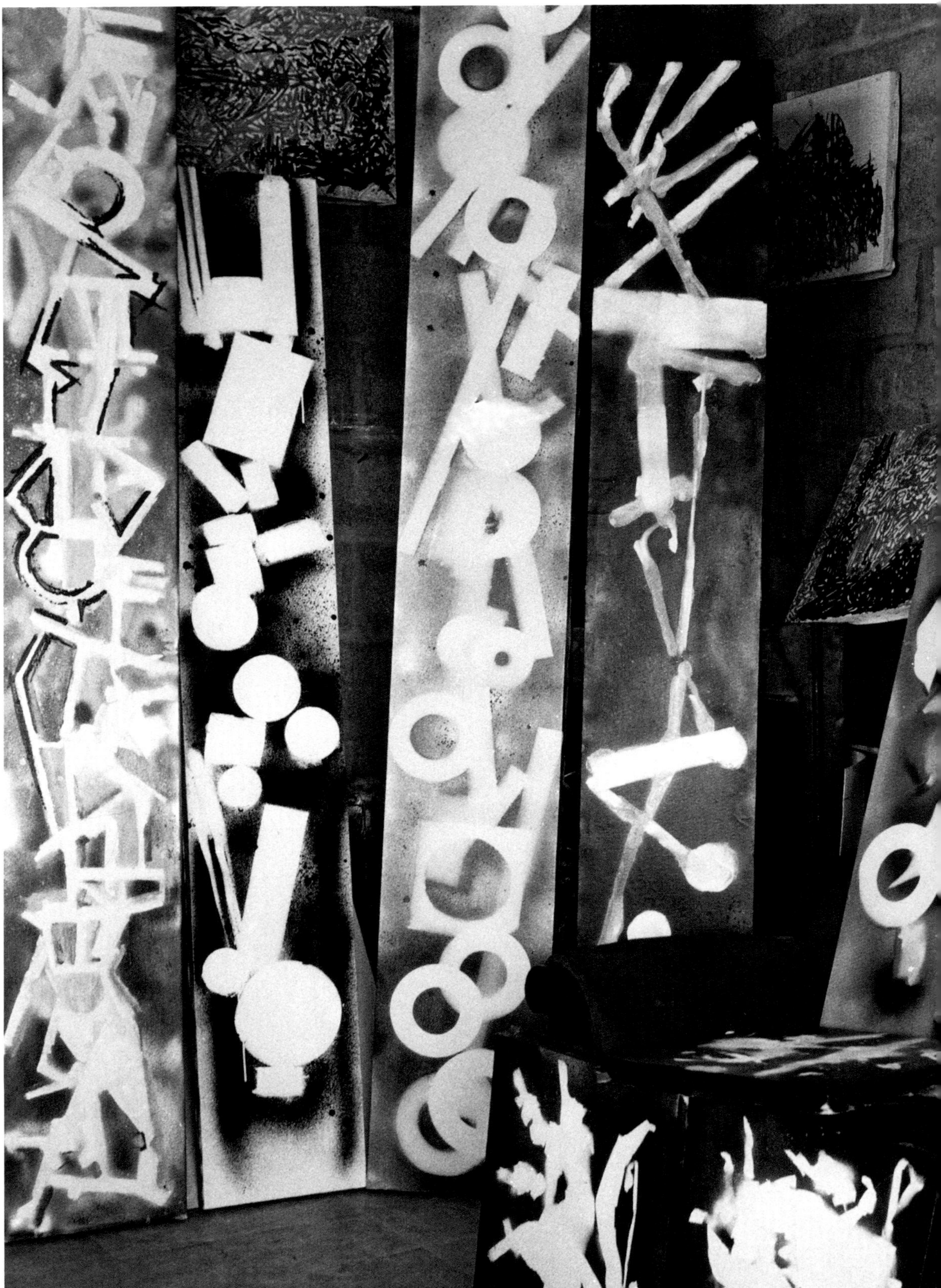

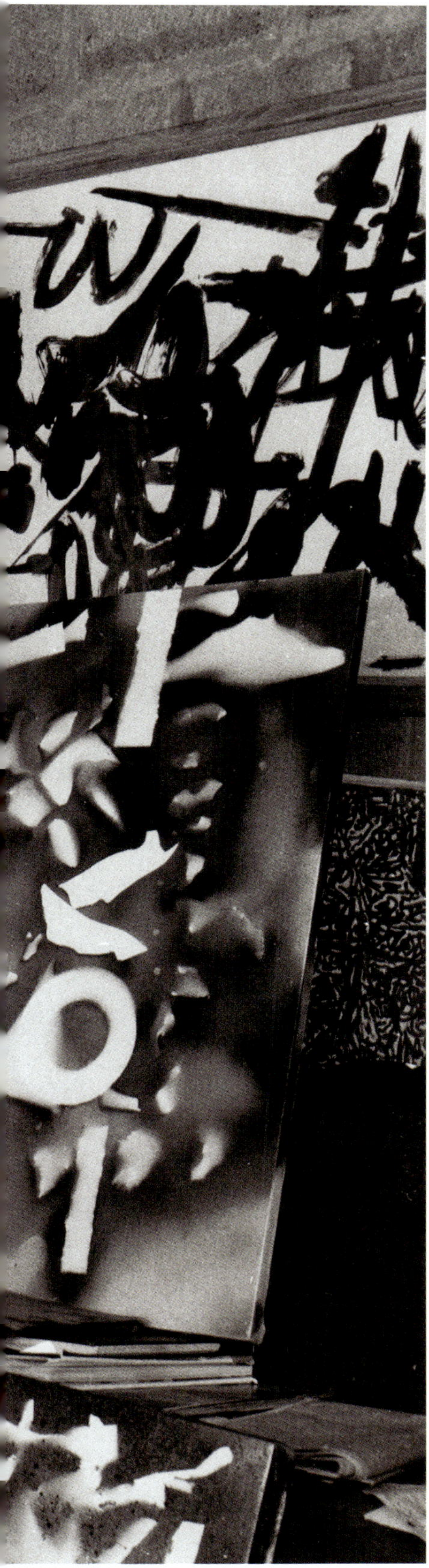

the Sprays. Smith and Kramer, who were working together on the *Arts* issue, knew the new paintings would likely not be well received. Smith wrote to Lois Orswell on July 8, 1959: "He [Kramer] thinks the painting show will upset things a bit – sculptors are not supposed to paint even painters think

"There is no conceptual difference between painting and sculpture. …The position of creating does not change…just because the medium changes."

so except for Matisse + Picasso – but sculptors are always for painters sculpture…."[18] As predicted, most critics were not enthusiastic, and nothing sold, yet Smith continued the Sprays until his death, creating a major body of work from 1957 to 1965 in this new medium.

Smith took full advantage of the *Arts* opportunity to publish the most complete statement to date of his working process and aesthetic vision.[19] The stunning conclusion to the section devoted to him in the February 1960 issue was a two-page spread of annotated photographs that connected his sculpture with his activity as a painter and draftsman. Facing a photograph of his living room floor covered with calligraphic brush and ink drawings and small Sprays was a picture of the recently finished *Bouquet of Concaves.* A cropped closeup of it unassembled outside the studio appeared as an inset on the same page. Smith drew

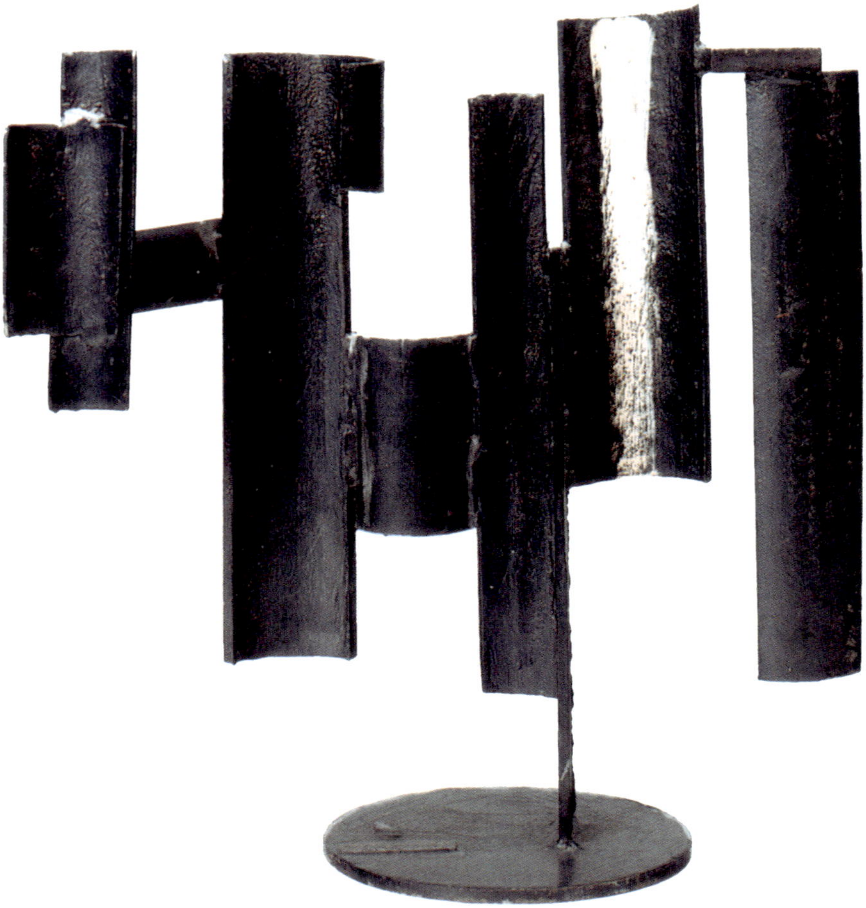

Bouquet of Concaves II, 1960, steel, painted

RIGHT: *Bouquet of Concaves*, 1959, photograph by David Smith

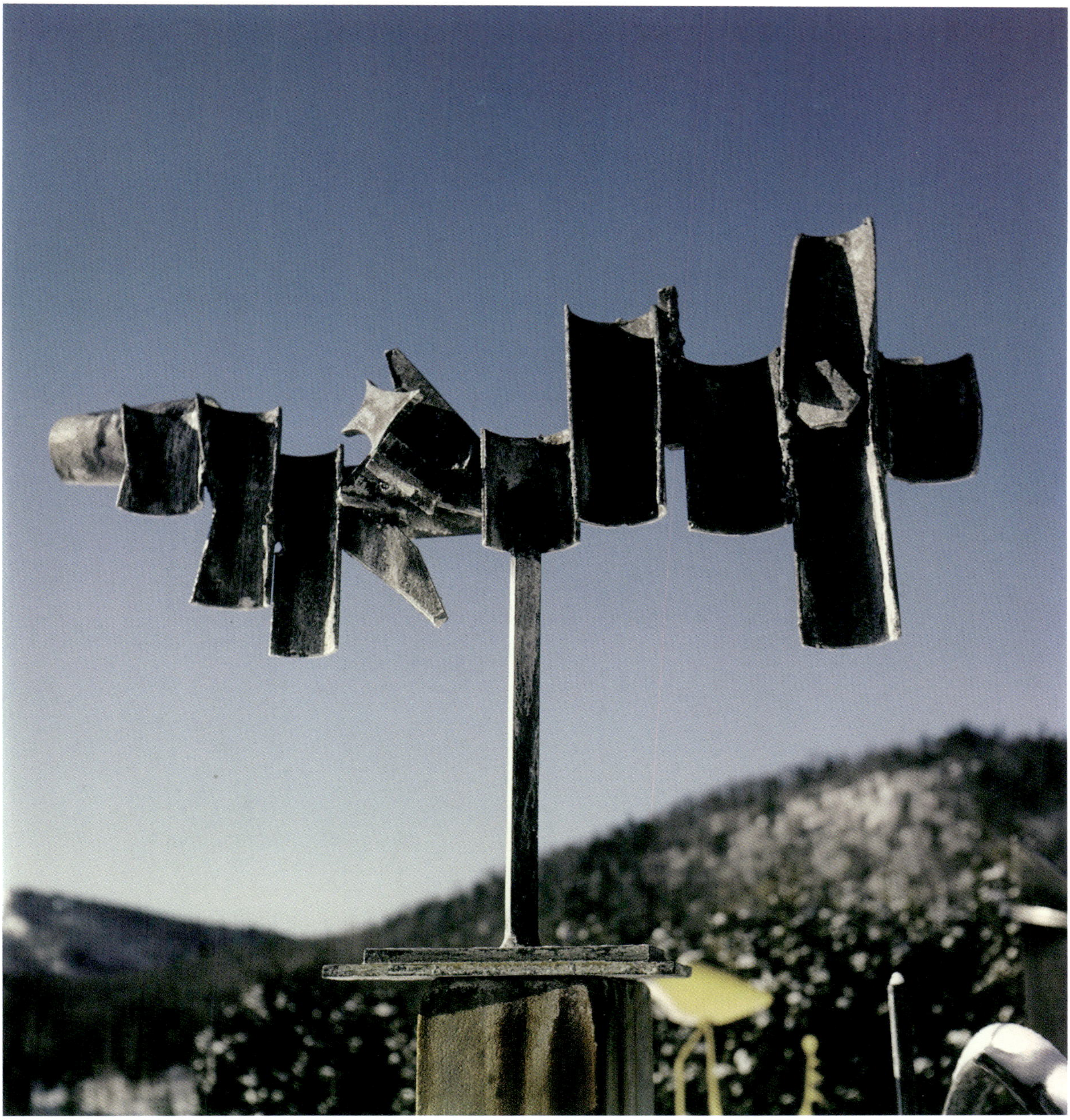

an arrow to the jumble of tubular forms that were little more than rough, irregular remnants of steel tubing and industrial steel waste and wrote "concaves," identifying for the interested reader a seminal element in his formal vocabulary (*pages 31, 47*).[20]

As recent scholarship has pointed out, certain formal motifs, like the circle, began to recur in Smith's sculpture in the 1950s, becoming essential to his style at a time when he was simplifying his forms into a more geometric vocabulary.[21] Around 1952, he became increasingly fascinated with concave and convex forms, which became a major part of his formal vocabulary for a decade. Central to the modernist tradition, they can be traced back to the earliest cubist experiments in the years before World War I. As Smith moved away from creating sculptures in predominantly open linear configurations, the rhythm of convex and concave forms allowed him to add volume without bulk or solid mass and gave him endless variations on volume, shape, line, and contour. It was one means of liberating sculptural form from its traditional strictures. As he wrote: "Form...doesn't need to be full rounded – indications function instead – permitting the sculpture on a whole to have varying and different aesthetic purposes."[22]

Concave and convex took hold of Smith's imagination in his series of Tanktotems, begun in 1952. The earliest ones, like *Tanktotem IV* (1953), are anthropomorphic personages composed of the slightly rounded boiler tank ends, which give the series its name, connected to narrow lengths of semicylindrical steel tubing (*page 34*). Later ones are more abstract in their principal emphasis on asymmetrical configurations of line and geometric shapes.

***Untitled (9/3/59)*, 1959, brush and black ink on wove paper**

BELOW: *Bouquet of Concaves*, 1959 photograph and annotations by David Smith, published in *Arts*, February 1960

NEXT: *Untitled*, c. 1951, ink and tempera on paper

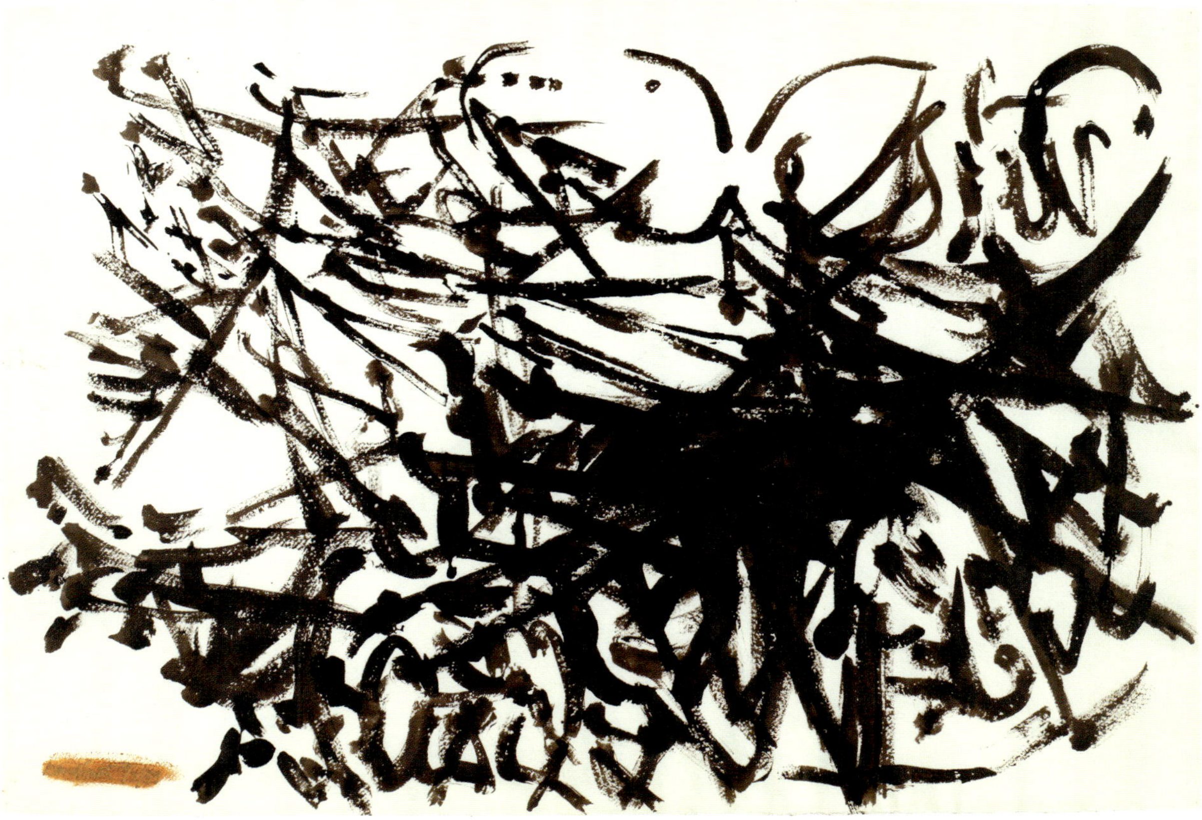

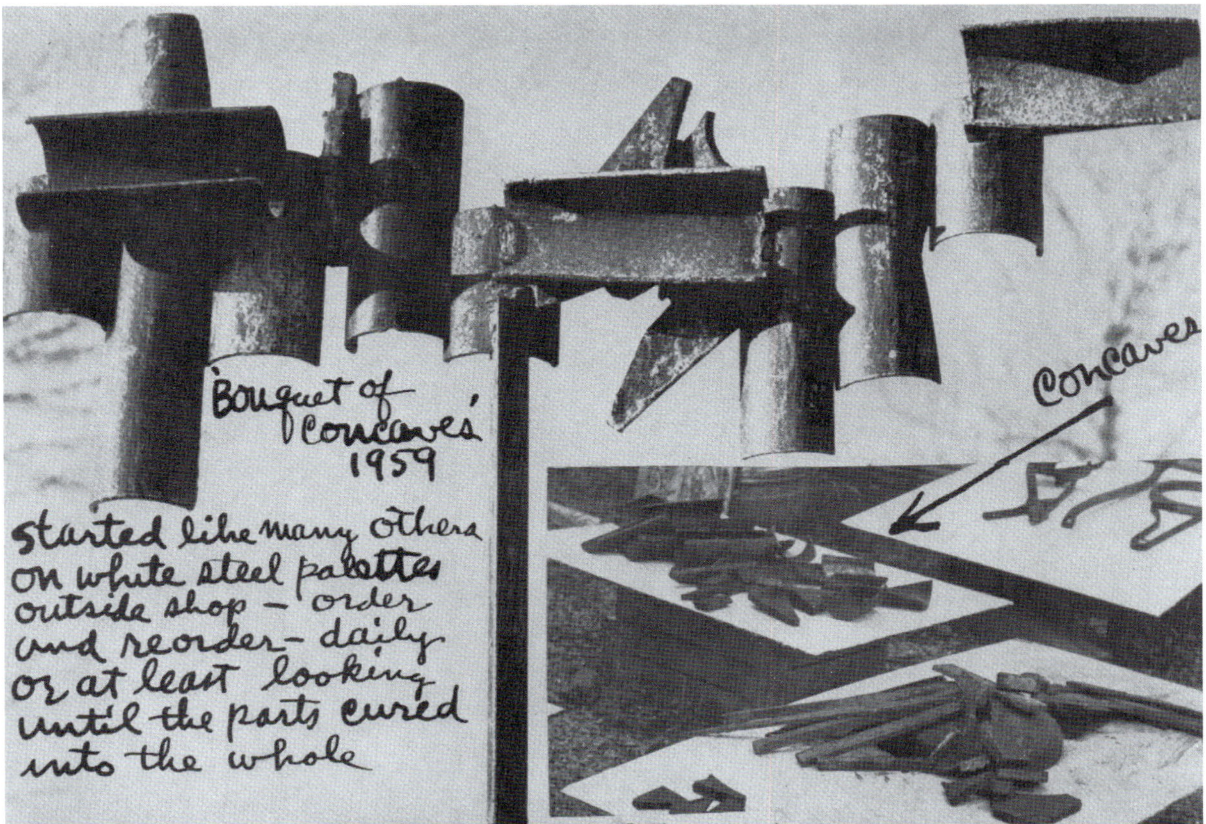
'Bouquet of Concaves' 1959
started like many others on white steel palettes outside shop – order and reorder – daily or at least looking until the parts cured into the whole
Concaves

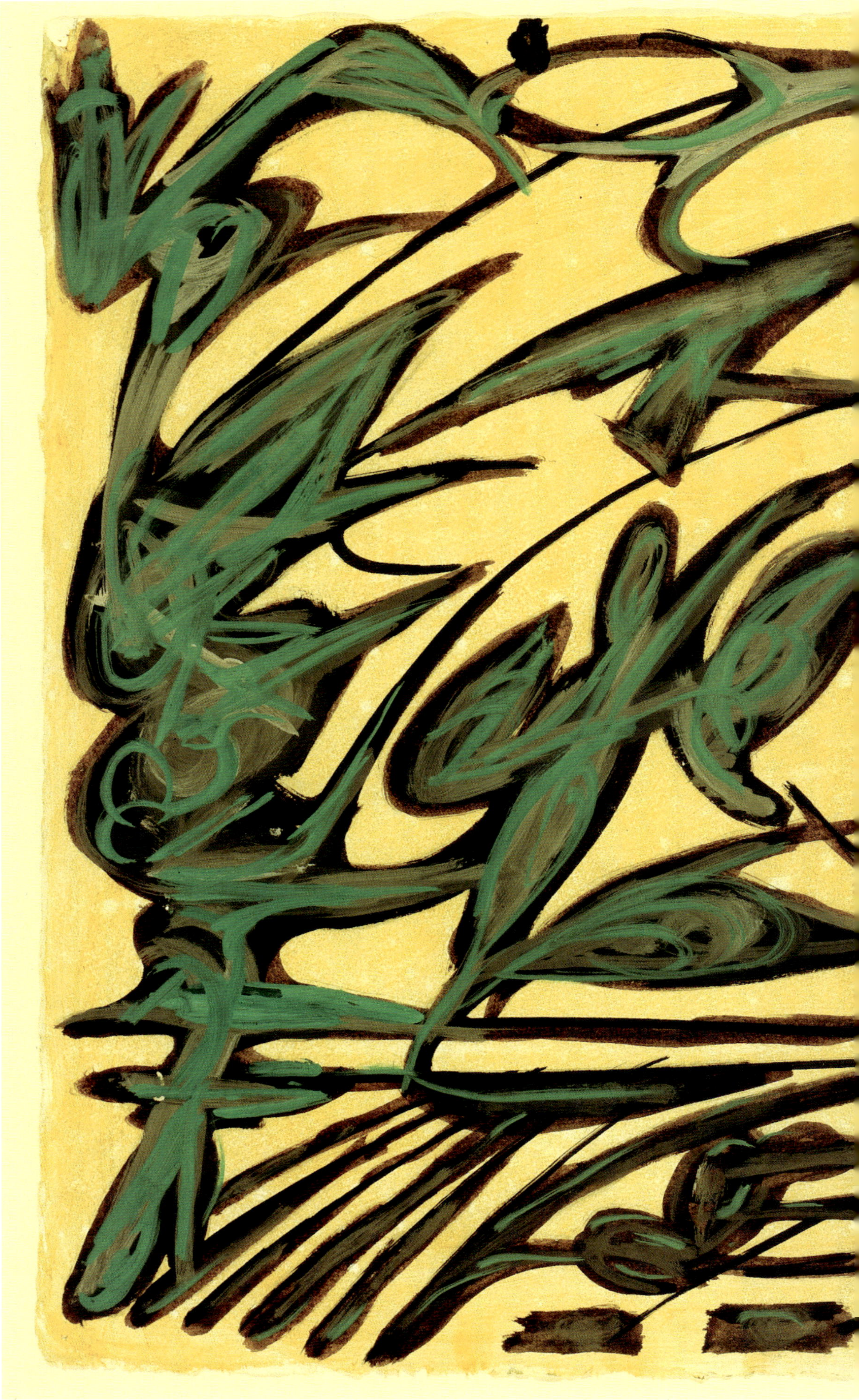

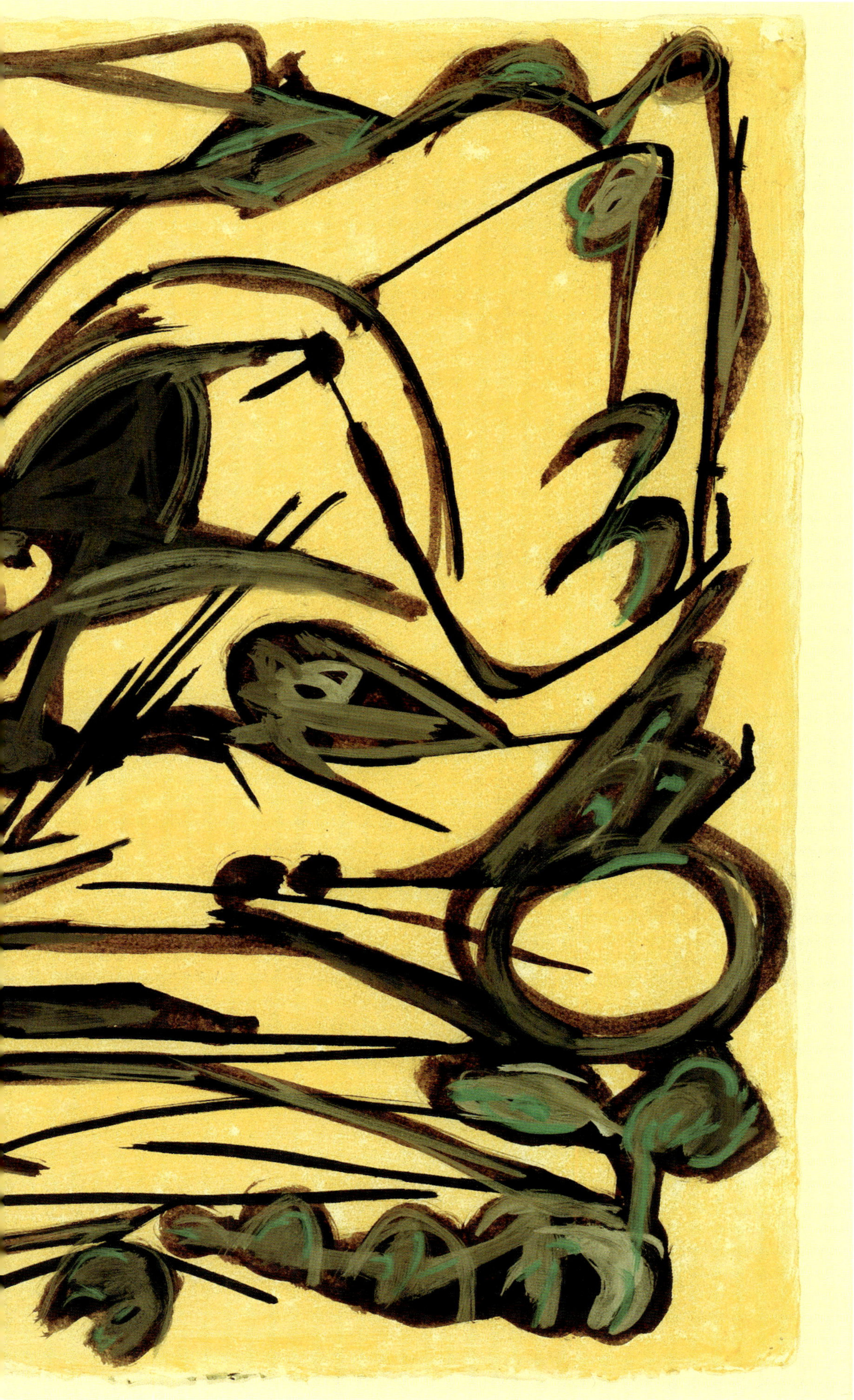

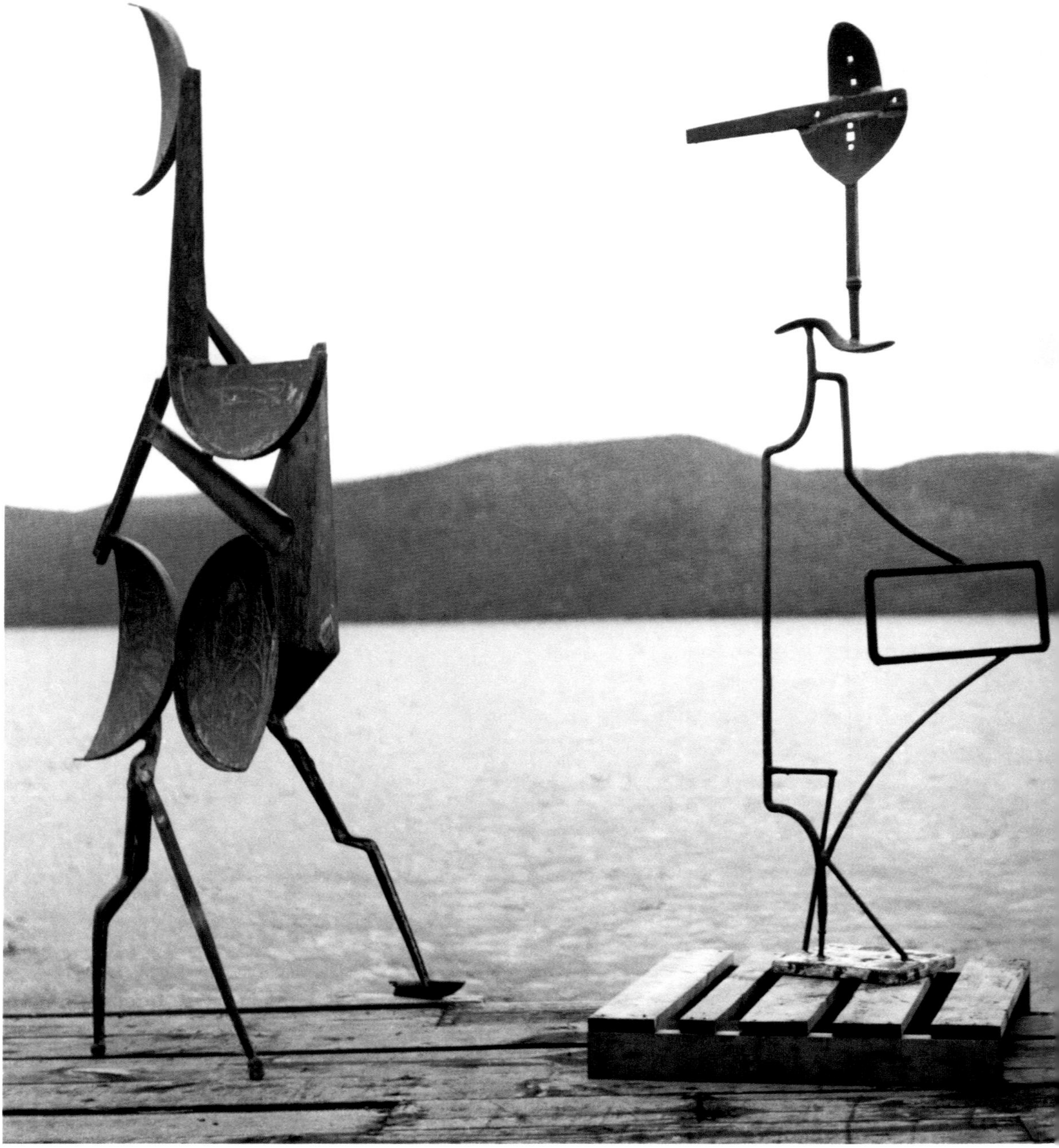

Tanktotem IV, 7/29/53, and *Tanktotem III* photographed by David Smith against Lake George, on the town dock at Bolton Landing, c. 1953

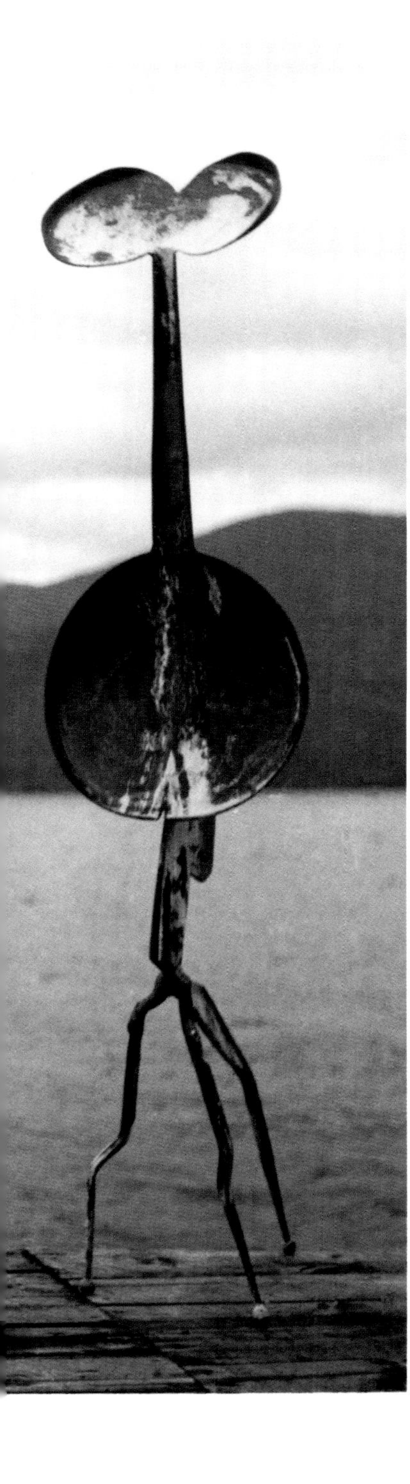

The long semi-cylindrical steel tubes and concave tank ends of *Tanktotem V* (1956) (*page 20*), for example, carefully balance diagonal lines against rectangles and circles, while *Tanktotem VI* (1957–59) (*page 36*) compresses these elements into a narrow column of curved versus straight, hollow versus round, solid versus void. The boiler tank tops that unite the Tanktotems afforded Smith a circular form that was different on each side and endlessly variable in its character, depending on its scale and on whether he cut it into new shapes.

Examples of the many variations of concave and convex that Smith employed can be found in other works. He incorporated the round boiler tank end into the Ravens with *Raven V* (1959) (*page 42*) and *August Raven* (1960), introducing a new motif into a series characterized by calligraphic tangles of solid steel bars (*page 70*). Concave and convex as volumetric form define the bronze figures *Personage of May* (1957), *Detroit Queen* (1957), and *Auburn Queen* (1959) (*pages, 38, 80*). Working in bronze allowed Smith to "collage" disparate materials and objects that could not be welded together. With this additive process he was able to create entirely new objects and experiment with greater depth and irregularity of volumetric form by working with found materials more forgiving than steel. *Auburn Queen*, for example, has a central slightly twisted hollow shaft that connects four voluminous curved forms to a conical base, whose linear patterns stand in distinct contrast to the boldness of the convex and concave forms used.[23] Smith described his train of thought as he worked as "simply all in the visual world, the language is image."[24] Known to be eclectic in his visual sources, Smith was interested in art from all periods and cultures.[25] Not only does *Auburn Queen* recall Picasso, but she is also the modern descendant of the tiny Minoan figurines of bare-breasted snake goddesses that Smith knew

"Form doesn't need to be full rounded. . .permitting the sculpture on a whole to have varying and different aesthetic purposes."

from ancient Greek art and his extended trip to Greece and Crete in the 1930s.[26]

At the same time that Smith was incorporating concave and convex forms into his figurative sculpture in the late 1950s, he was shifting to standing, geometric, relief-like sculptures that offered other opportunities to explore the character and range of concave form. This is particularly apparent in small-scale works from 1959 to 1961 that focused on the semi-cylindrical and the planar, in both the 1959 and 1960 versions of *Bouquet of Concaves* (*pages 28, 29*), *Black Concaves* (1960) (*page 41*), and *Bolton Landing* (1961). In many ways these were formally connected in Smith's mind to Fernand Léger's experiments in the series Contrastes de formes (1912–14).[27]

In the first *Bouquet of Concaves*, Smith moved away from anthropomorphism to explore more abstract relationships of convexity and concavity. For the *Bouquet*, he used the trope of flowers on a stem or, as his photographs of it suggest, a bird's wing. Translating the traditional pictorial concerns of Western still life painting into sculpture, he used contrasting textures, surfaces, and form in

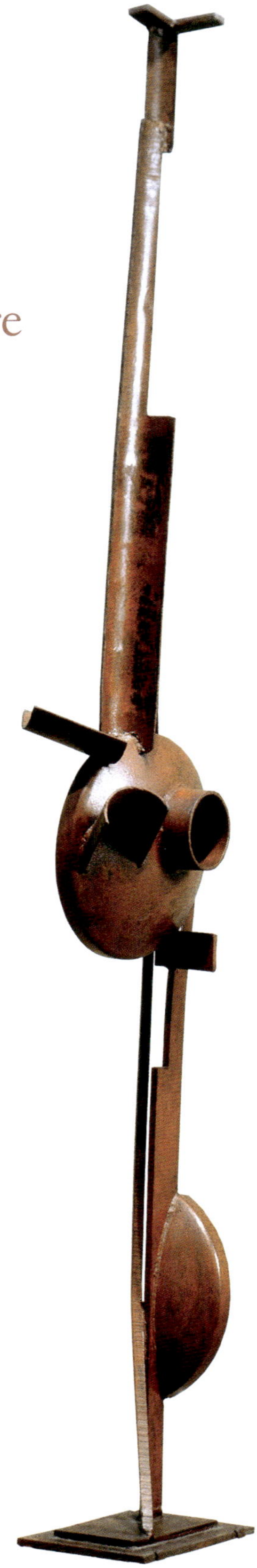

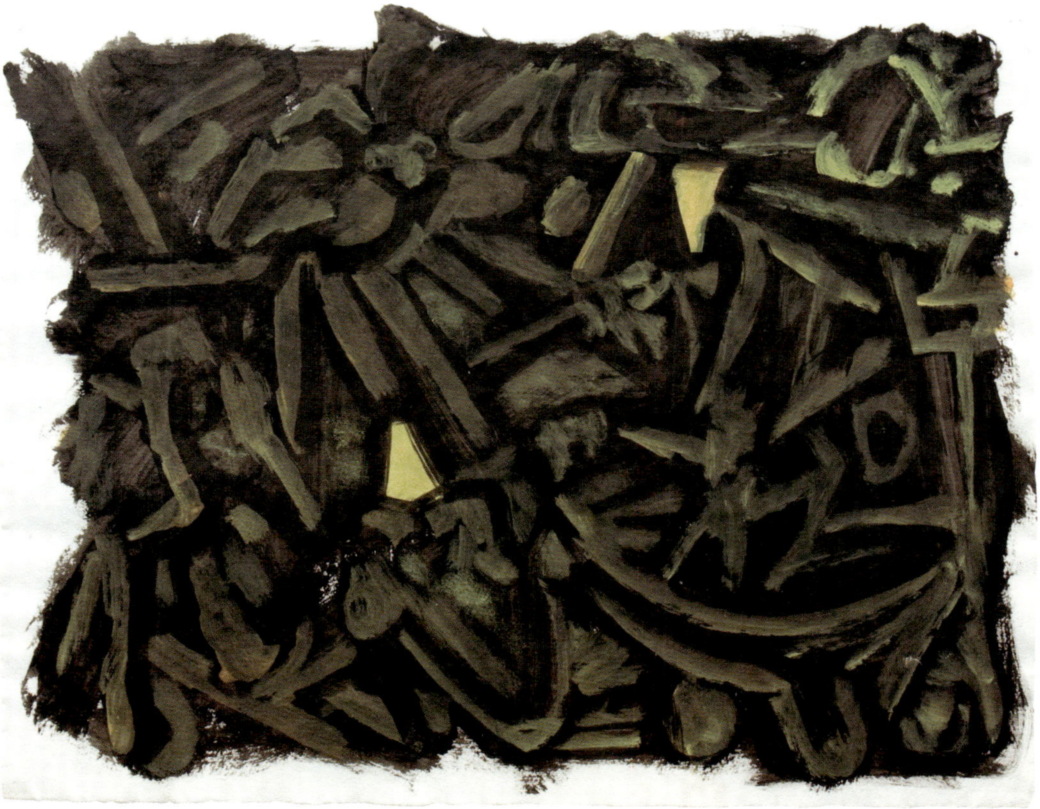

a way quite different from Picasso's approach in *Glass of Absinthe* (1914), one of the earliest examples of still-life sculpture in the modern era.[28] The original identity of the rough steel forms that make up the *Bouquet* is unclear, allowing them to function abstractly as contour, edge, hollow, round, and surface. A sophisticated writer and poet, Smith knew that the word "bouquet" carried suggestions of nature and impermanence, even softness, as well as the notion of perfume. His *Bouquet*, however, upends those traditional associations with the coarseness of its hard steel concaves even as they are structured pictorially like a profusion of blossoms in a vase.

Smith argued that there was no conceptual difference between painting and sculpture. As he put

***Tanktotem VI*, 1957, steel, painted**

ABOVE: *Untitled*, 1957, Egg tempera on paper

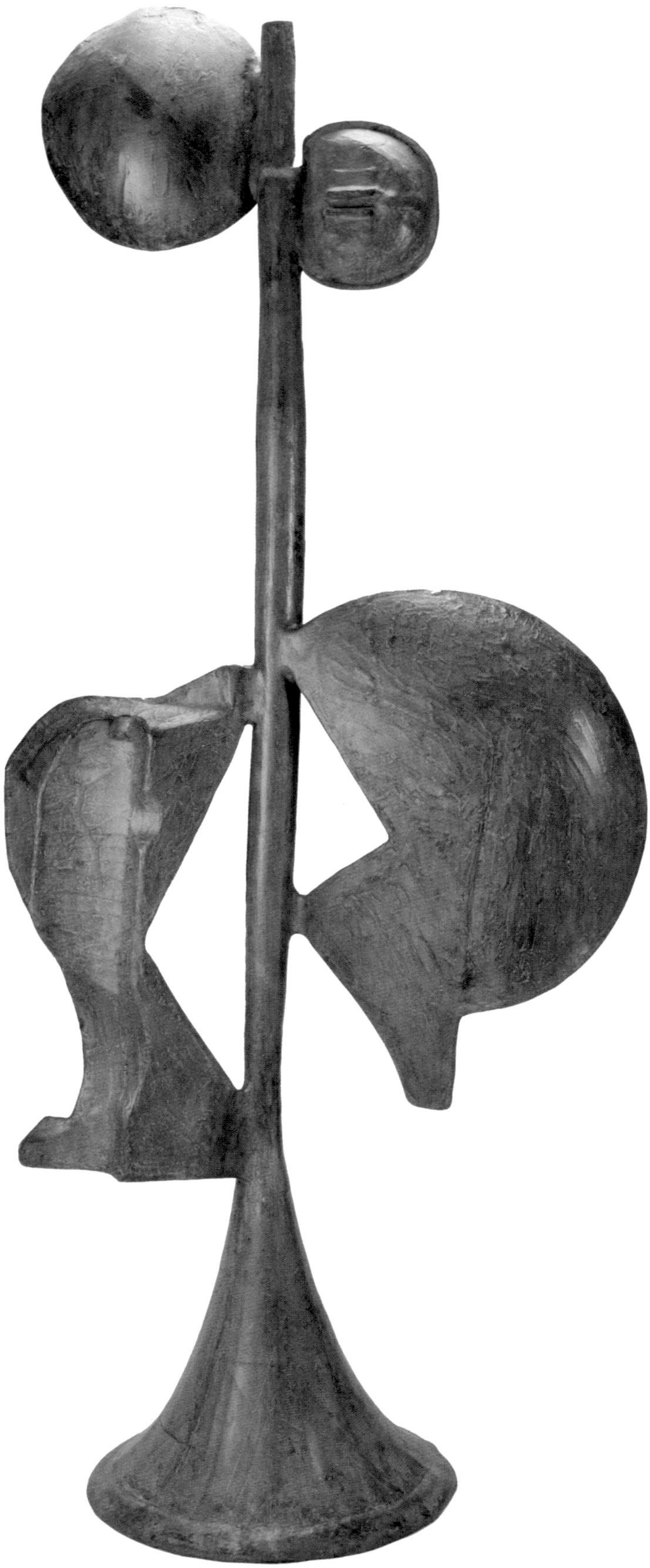

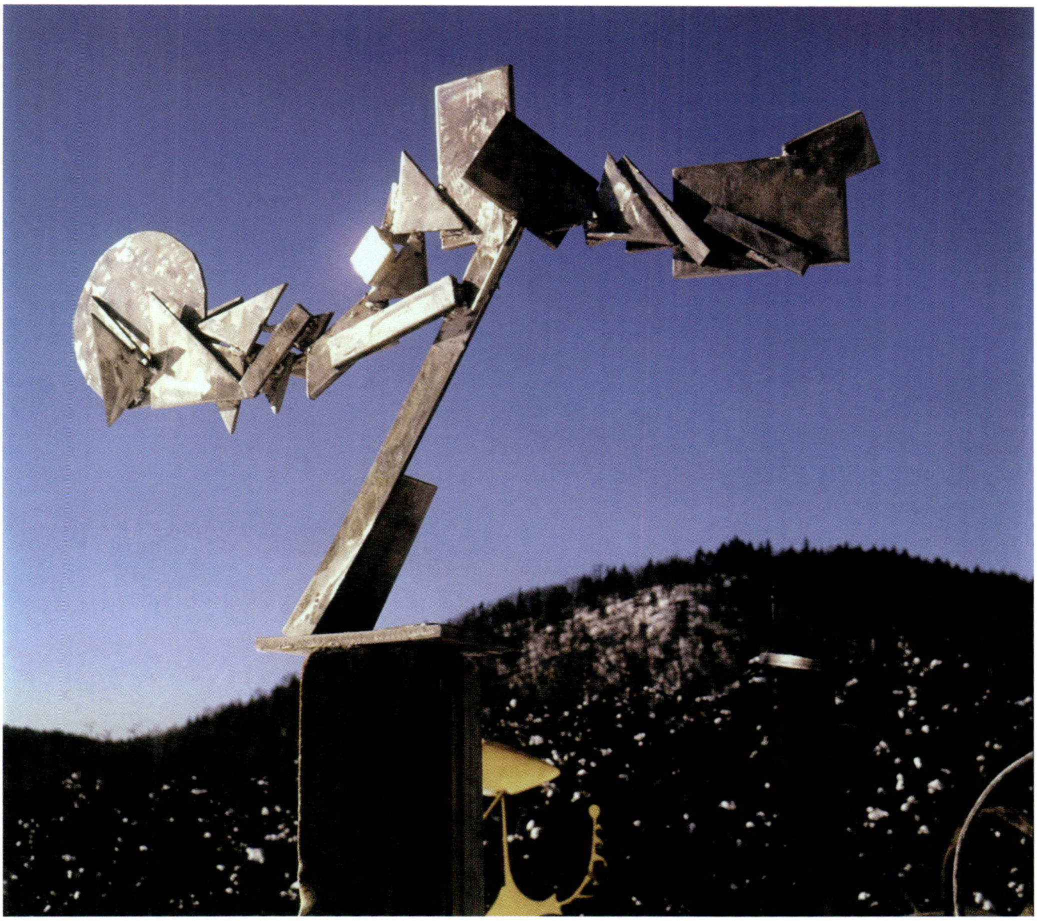

it: "The position of creating does not change...just because the medium changes."[29] The pictorial quality of the *Bouquet of Concaves* (*page 83*), its rigid horizontal alignment and relationship of parts to whole, relates not only to Smith's painting, but shares a compositional and formal syntax with Robert Motherwell's monumental painting series known as Elegies to the Spanish Republic. Smith, who was close to Motherwell, maintained an aesthetic dialogue in his oeuvre similar to Motherwell's. Both artists were concerned with the rhythm of repeating shapes, often as formal opposites, balanced against each other within carefully structured formats that allowed for controlled experimentation.[30]

***Auburn Queen*, 1959, bronze**

ABOVE: *Circles and Angles*, 1959, photograph by David Smith

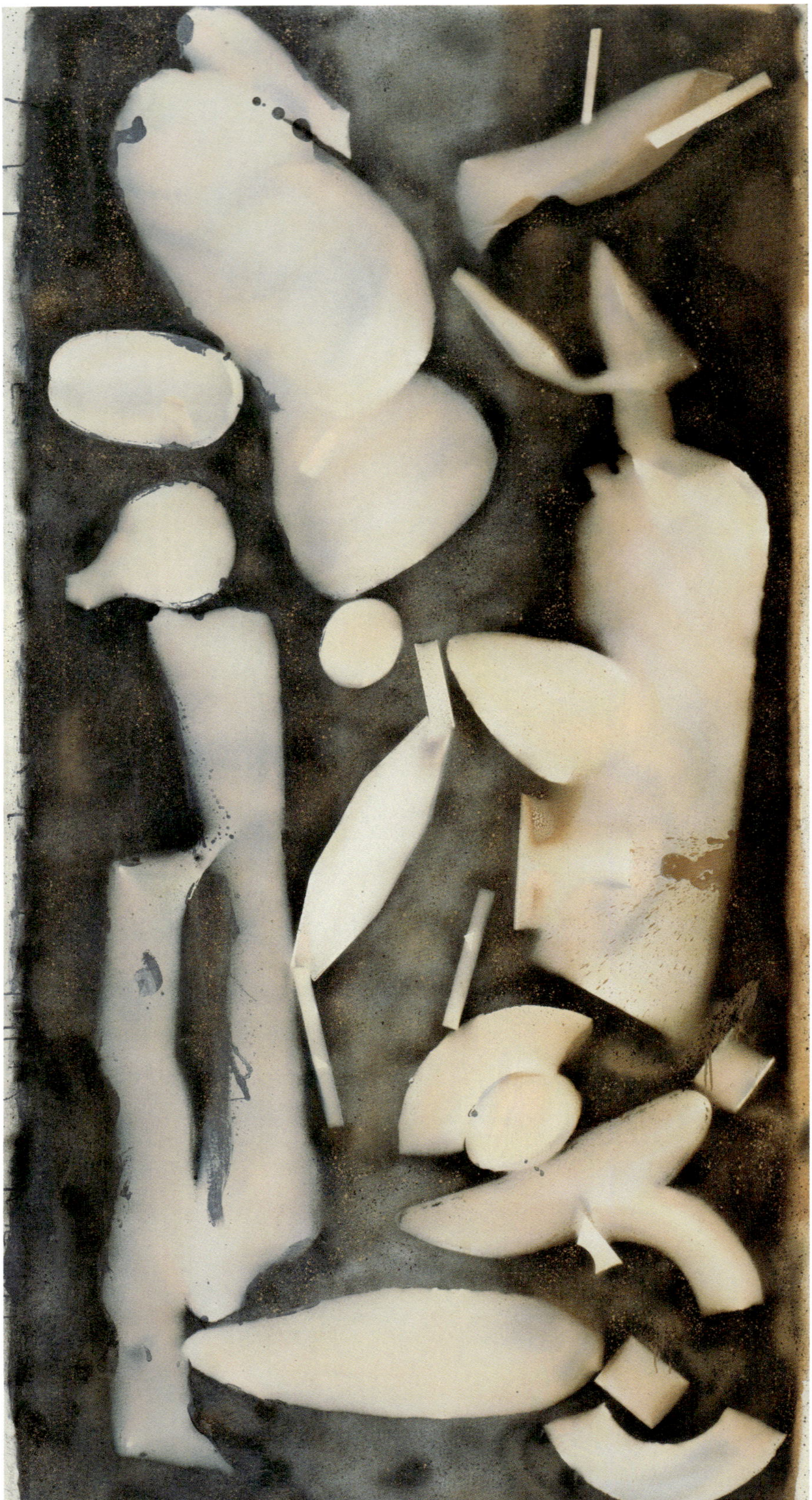

In a 1959 speech, Smith related how each of his sculptures "has a relationship to the work before, it is in continuity with the previous work – it often holds a promise or a gesture toward the one to follow."[31] The *Bouquet of Concaves* left a powerful imprint on Smith's visual memory. It suggested, he wrote, unities of "concaves in orders I had not found in my previous concaves."[32] With new configurations still to be explored, Smith pursued the series further in 1960 with *Bouquet of Concaves II* and the related *Black Concaves* (*pages 28, 52, 53*). He was also inspired to return to the Tanktotems for the first time in three years, creating in 1960 four sophisticated versions (VII, VIII, IX, and X) (*page 50*) that explore abstract relationships of color, circle, line, and plane in expressively painted configurations.[33] As he explained in a later interview, he would continue to work on the Tanktotems "as long as concave and convex are still a mystery."[34]

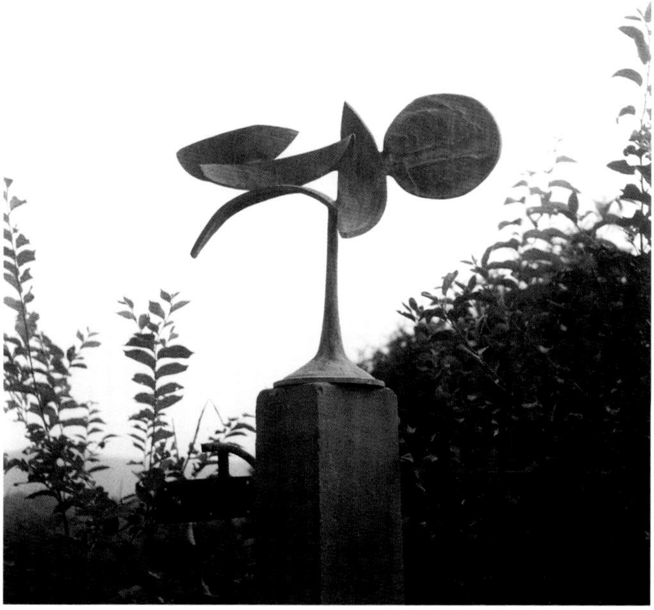

***First Ovals*, 1958, spray enamel on canvas**

RIGHT: *Bolton Landing*, 1961, photograph by David Smith

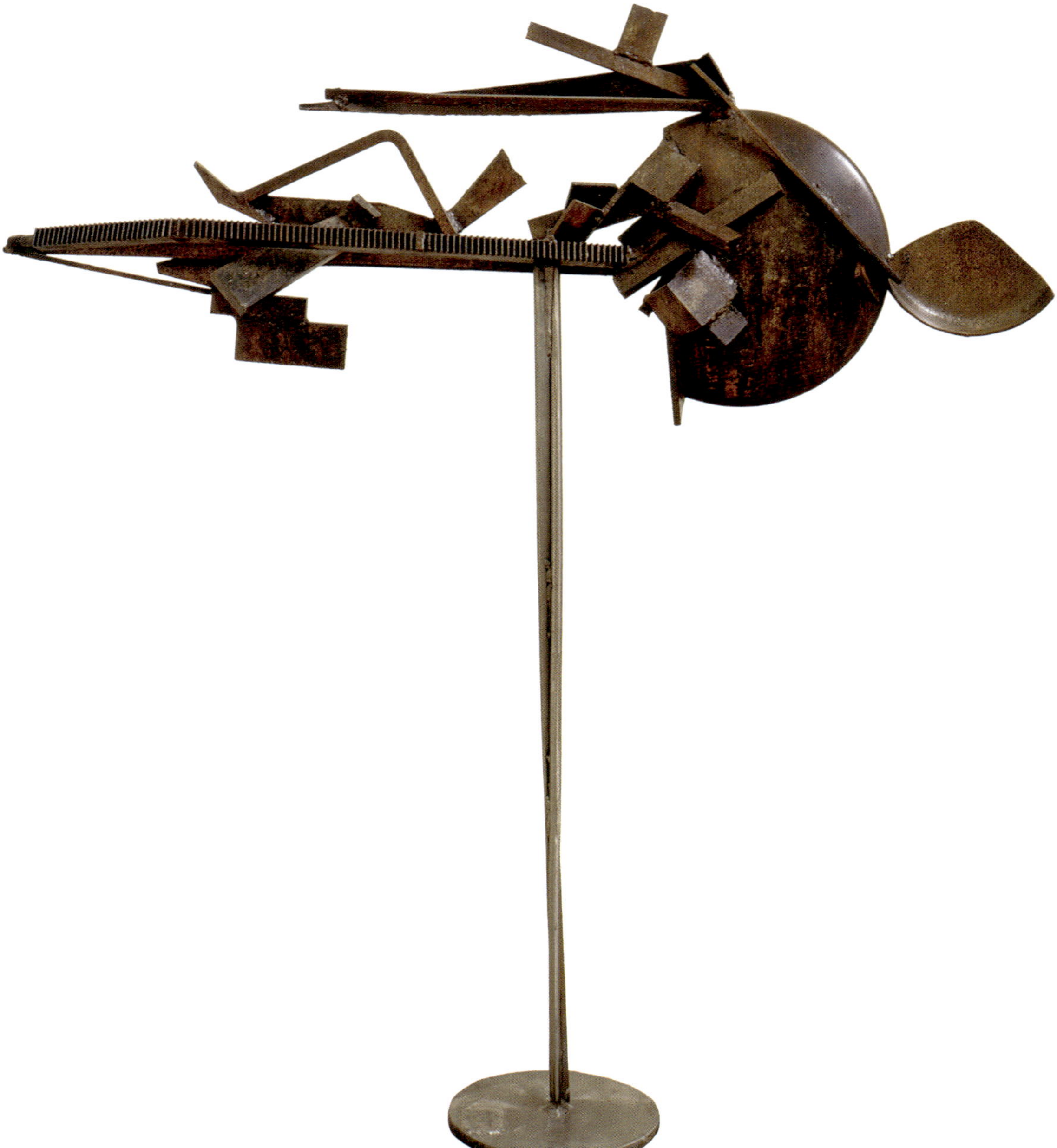

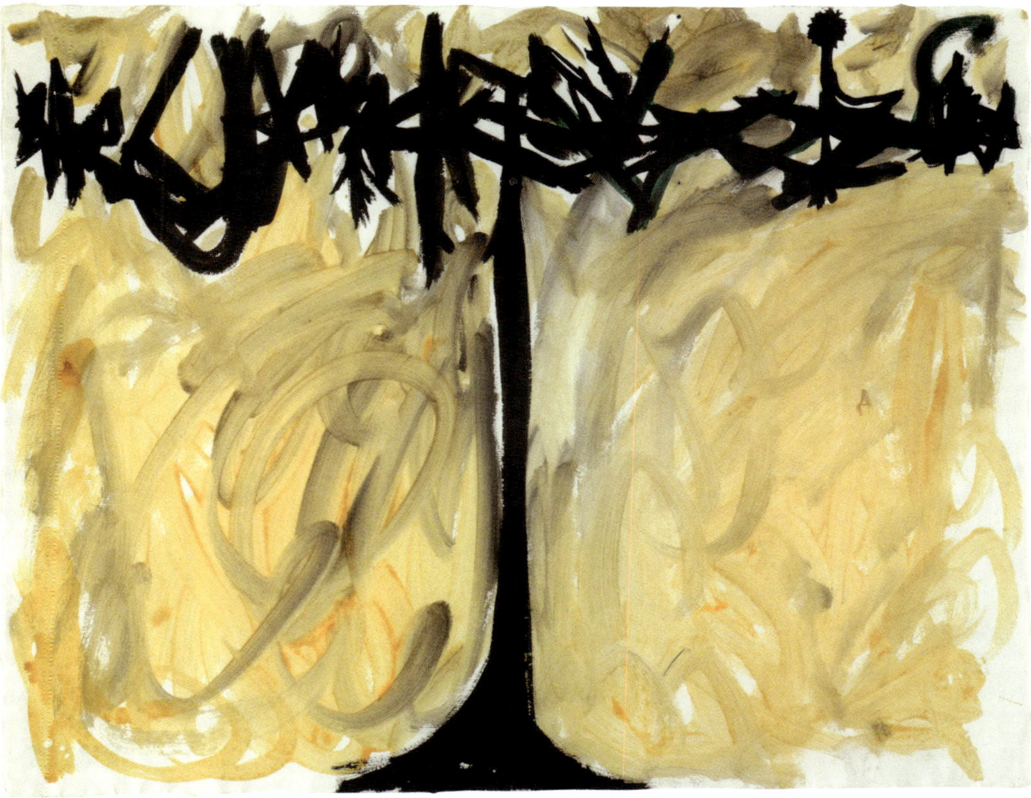

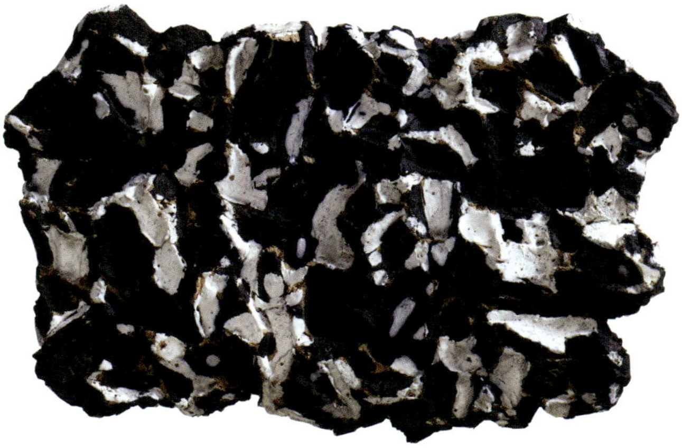

Raven V, 1959, steel

ABOVE: *Untitled*, 1950, black and yellow egg ink and green ink on paper

RIGHT: *Untitled*, 1955, clay

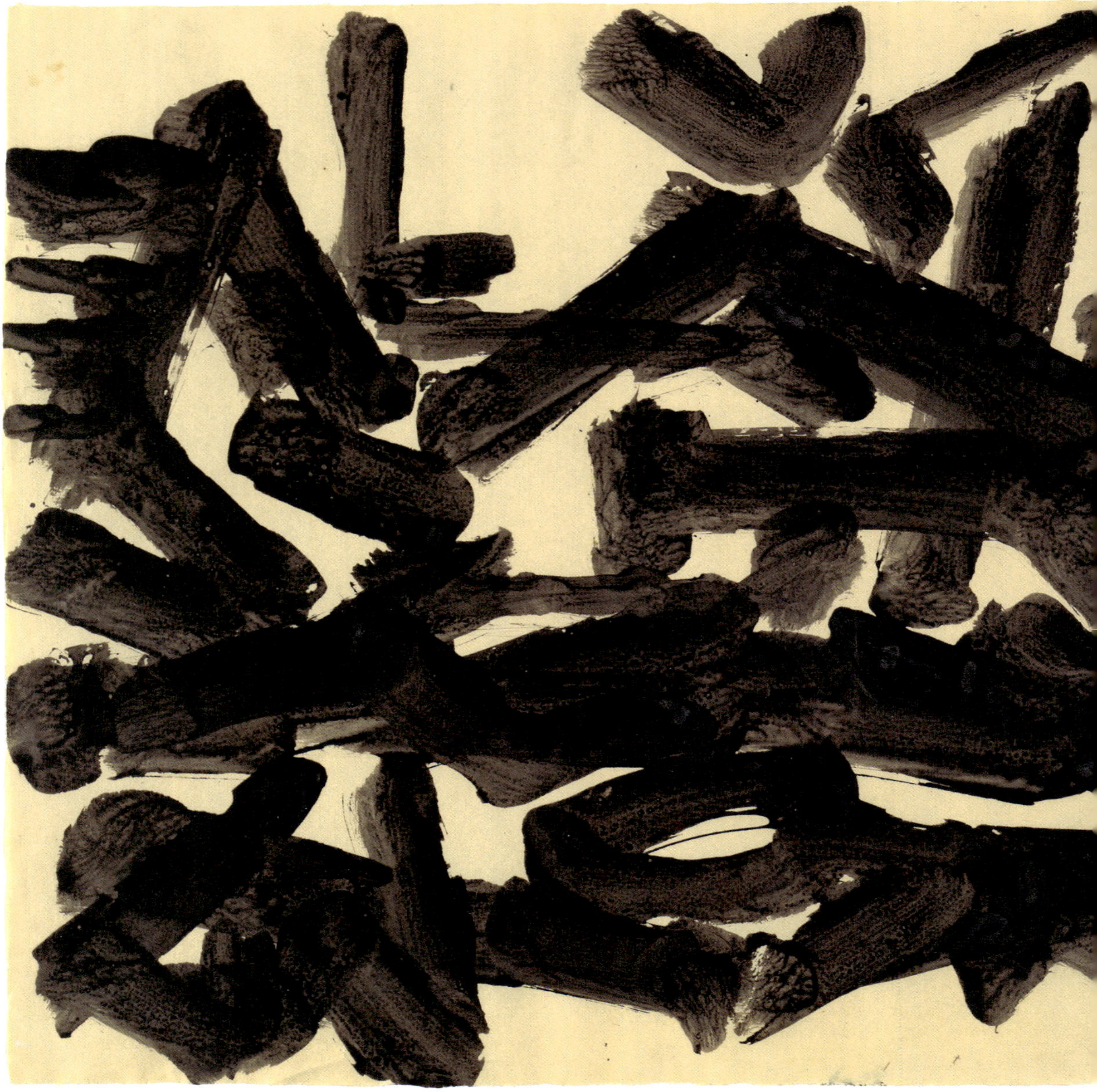

Untitled (11-22-58),
1958, brush and
black ink and egg
yolk on laid paper

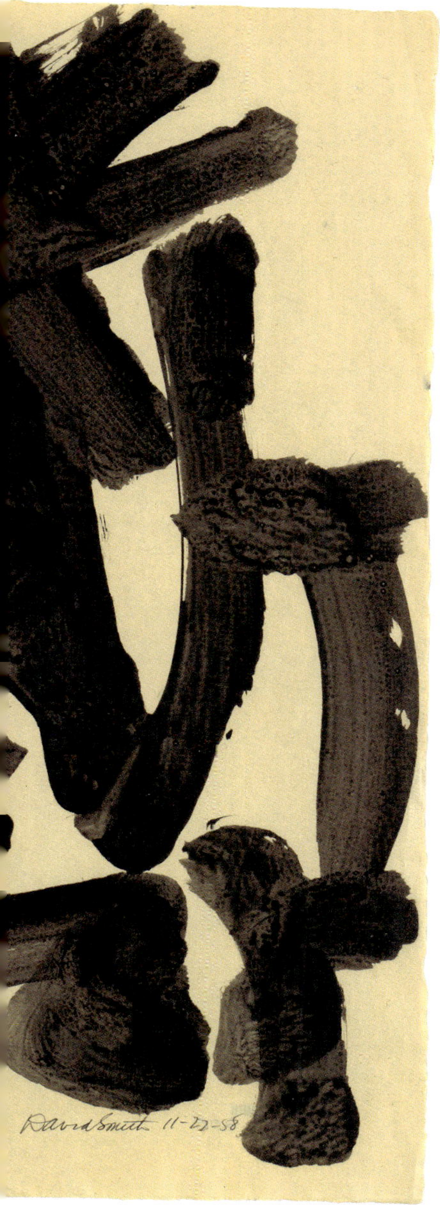

In *Bouquet of Concaves II* Smith experimented with convex and concave as an architectural configuration, balancing their contrasts in alternating vertical intervals. Its arrangement clearly relates to an earlier motif in one of Smith's drawings that imagines a sculptural construction as a series of linked pictorial vignettes. *Bouquet of Concaves II* also looks forward to a similar alternating arrangement of concave and convex semi-cylindrical

"Sculptors are not supposed to paint even painters think so except for Matisse + Picasso – but sculptors are always for painters sculpture...."

forms as a stepped vertical configuration in combination with flat cut-out shapes in the large-scale *Primo Piano II* (1962) (*pages 52, 53*).[35]

Smith affirmed in the special *Arts* issue of 1960 that even though he worked mostly in three dimensions, he "chewed the fat with painters."[36] As critic Frank O'Hara observed in 1961, Smith's sculpture is "never sculpture *being* painting, it is sculpture looking at painting and responding in its own fashion."[37] The pink stripes painted into two of the recessed concaves of *Bouquet II*, for example, bring to mind Barnett Newman's "zips," those agitated vertical stripes that divide his paintings and suggest three-dimensional space.[38] Smith's *Black Concaves* (1960) presents each side as a completely separate painted form, color and, surface treatment generating the object's dynamism. The pink stripe pops out from a black field of carefully balanced shapes on the convex side, while the shallow concaves appear to catch reflections and hold them permanently on the other side.

Smith did not believe there were any rules governing sculpture.[39] His refusal to treat three-dimensional form in the conventional manner, as something to be understood in the round, is a signature element of his work, resulting in radically different views in his sculpture. As early as 1952 he stated: "I don't see it from five different angles at once. I see one view. The round is only a series of fronts."[40] As he began to use color more boldly in 1960, pictorial illusionism became an important aspect of his sculptural form. Different sides of a work might receive totally different treatments, enhancing or denying the concavity of form, as in *Black Concaves* or *Tanktotem VII*, or color might be used to pick out the different concave and convex forms, emphasizing the shapes as separately

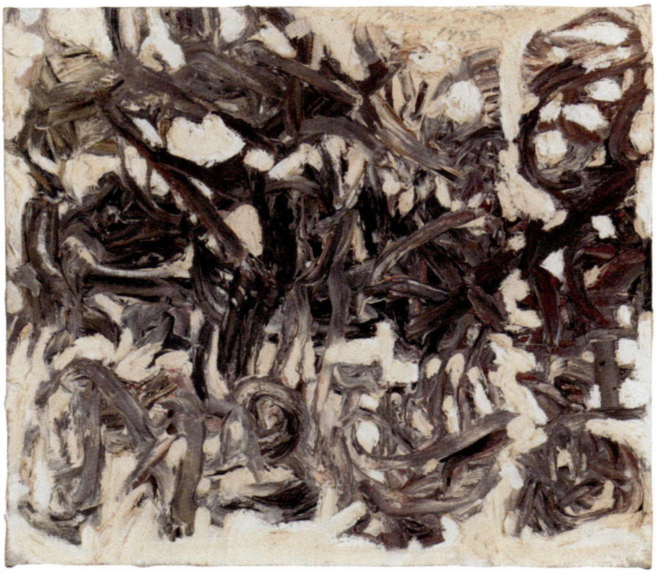

LEFT: ***Untitled***, **1956, oil on canvas**

ABOVE: ***Untitled***, **1957, spray enamel and oil on canvas**

BELOW: ***Bouquet of Concaves***, **1959, and** ***August Raven***, **1960, in progress outside workshop, photograph by David Smith, 1959**

NEXT: ***Untitled (Relief Painting)***, **1956, plaster and oil on canvas, on wood**

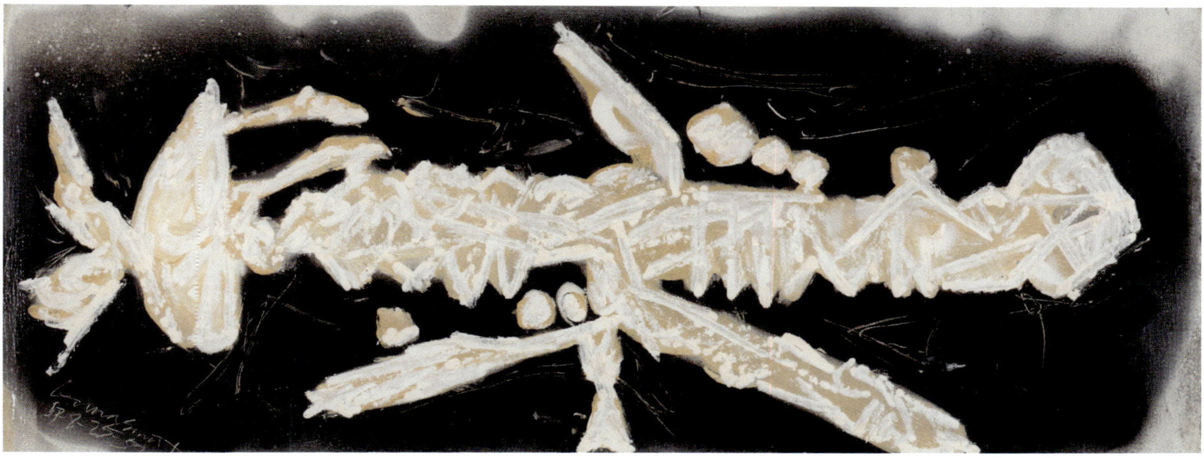

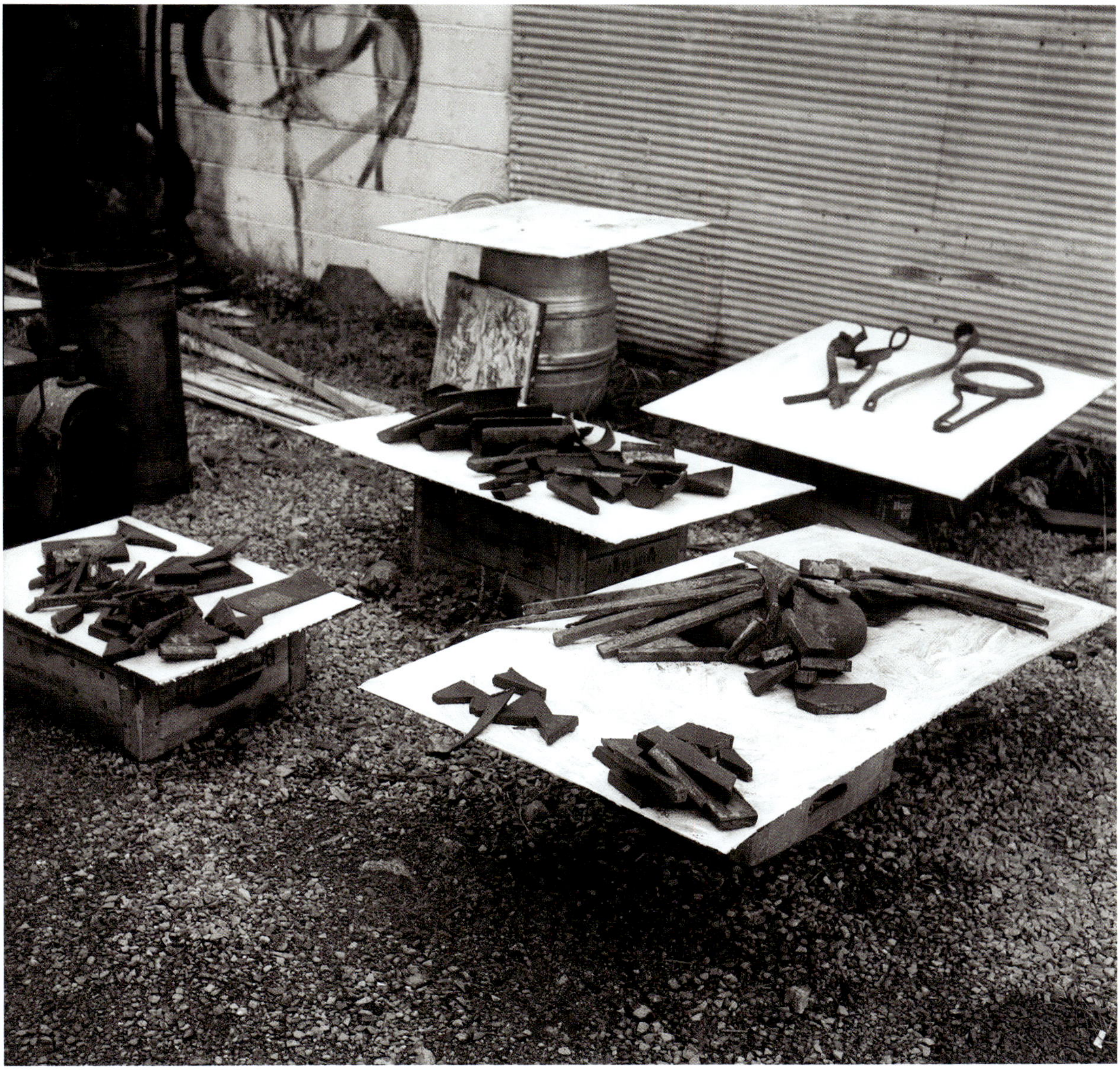

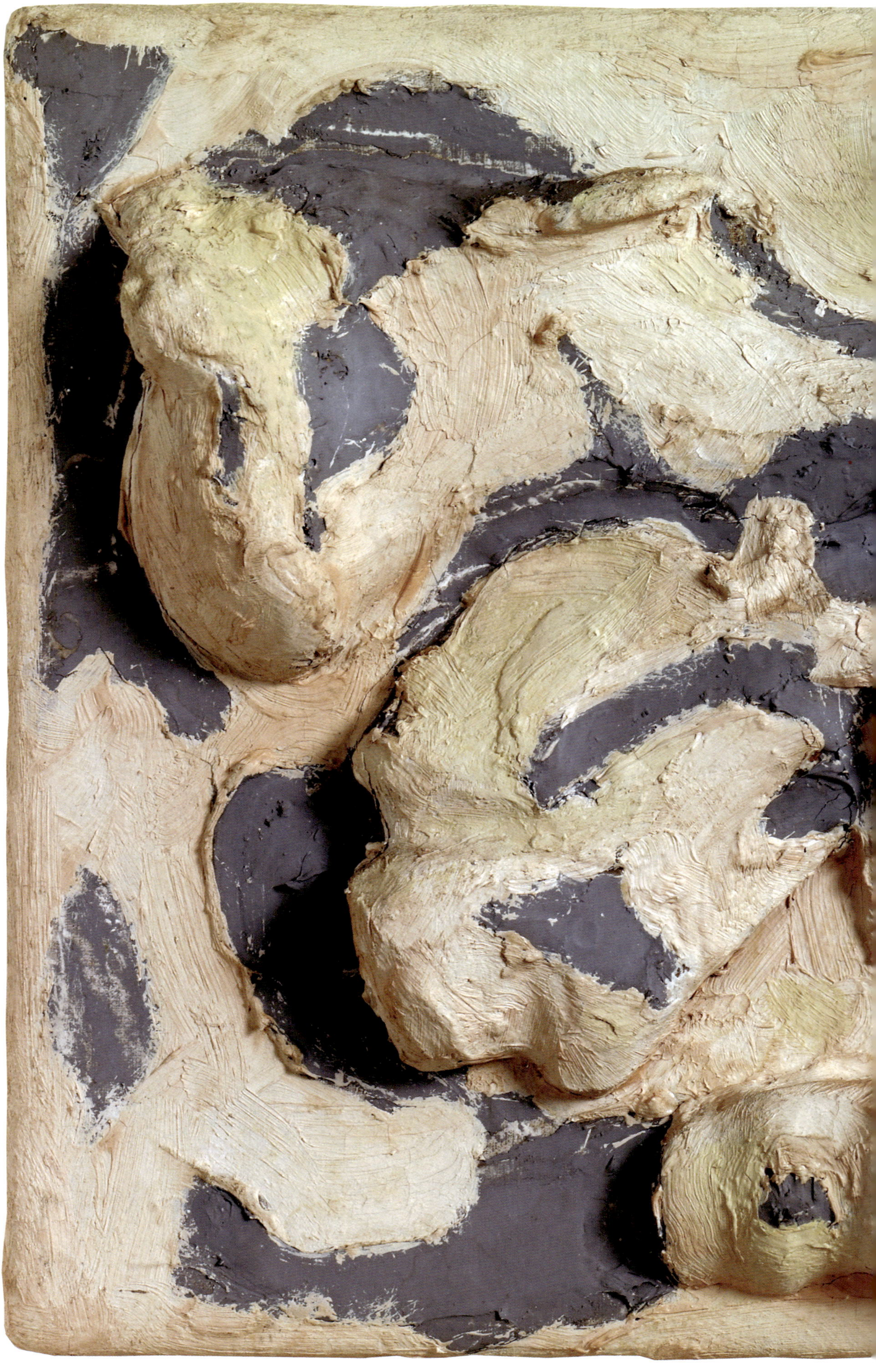

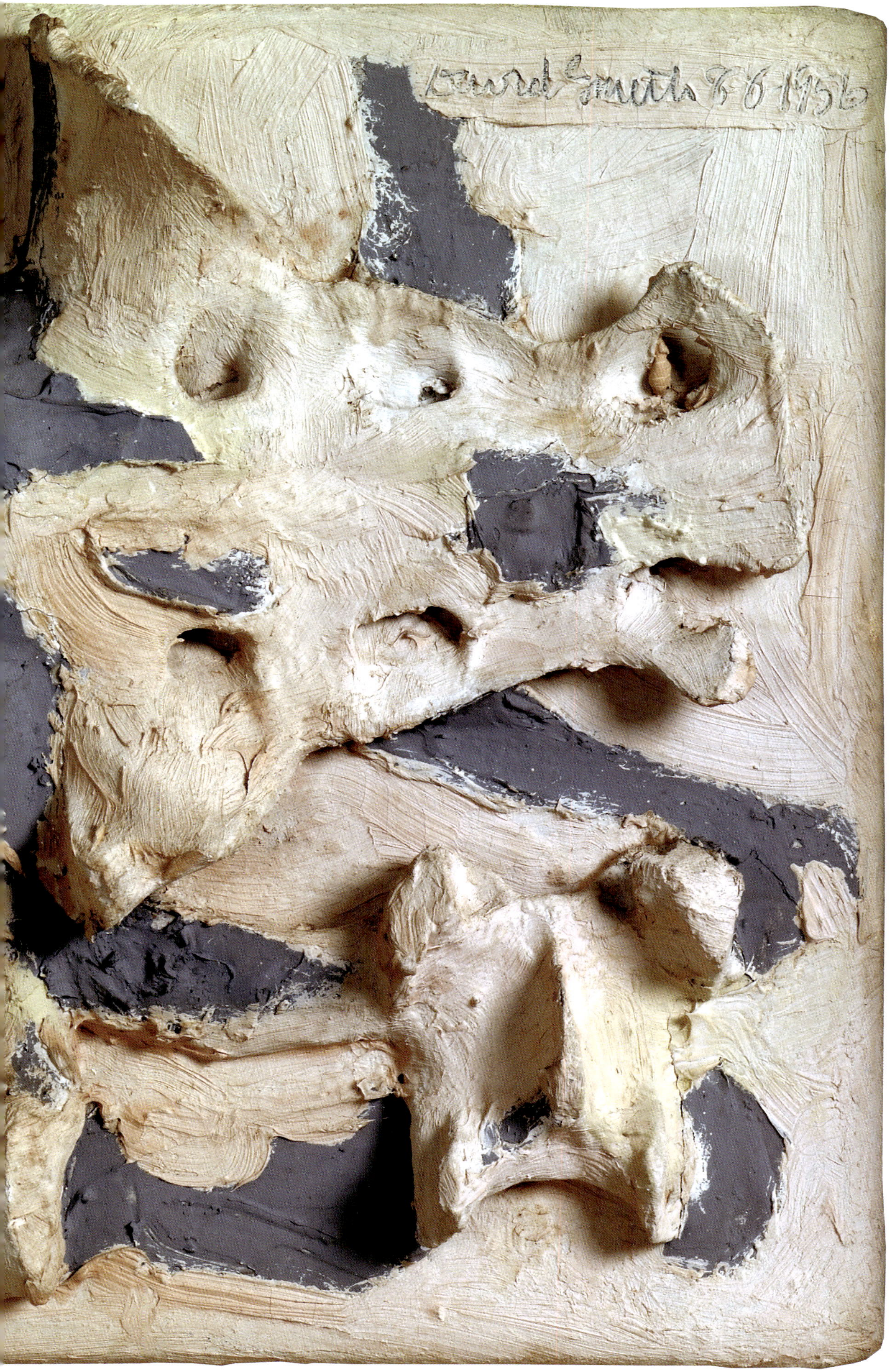
David Smith 8 6 1956

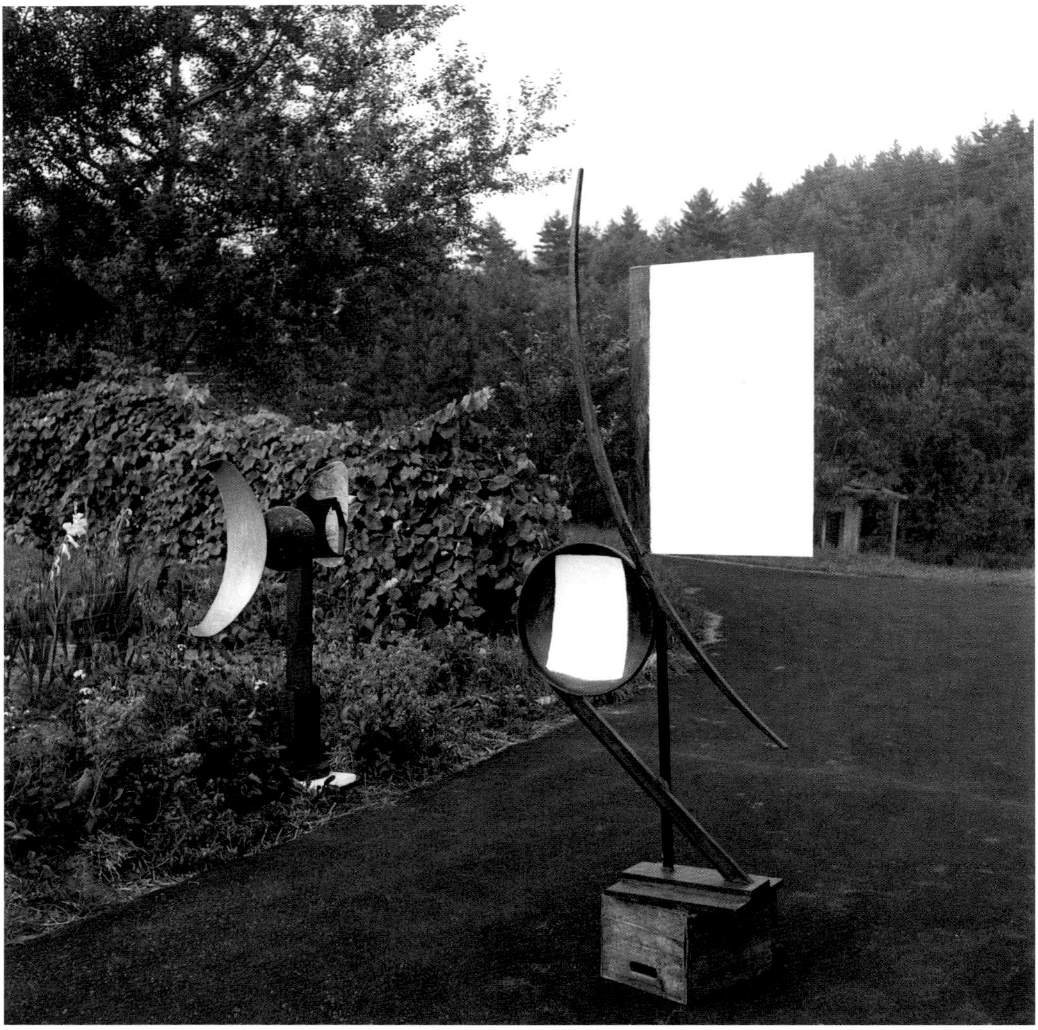

colored elements, as in *Tanktotem X*. Others have painted surfaces modeled with color, using brushwork that reveals vibrating colors beneath. In each case, Smith brushed on paint in a scumbled, gestural manner, turning the structured form into a three-dimensional painting.

Smith's articulated vision for "concaves larger than my own being" in unities and orders not found in "previous concaves," culminates with the monumentally scaled Zigs (1961–64), particularly the five completed in 1961. Using welded steel pipes of varying diameter – up to twenty-four

***Tanktotem X* and *Tanktotem VII*, photograph by David Smith, c. 1960**

RIGHT: *Night Window*, 1959, spray enamel on canvas

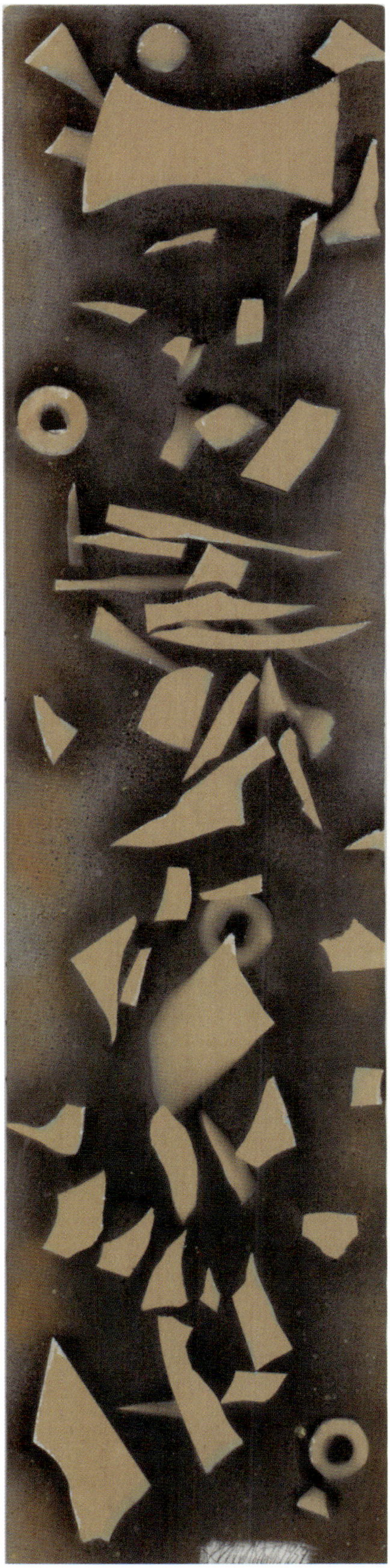

inches – Smith cut the oversized tubes into semi-cylindrical planes of varying length and width and combined them with I-beams or steel cut-outs that he made himself.[41] These multi-part structures, often over eight feet high, occupied real space and were radical experiments in color and form. Smith's ambition to compose on a monumental scale was achieved in the Zigs' complex

"Never sculpture being painting, it is sculpture looking at painting and responding in its own fashion."

formal relationships of curved planar concaves juxtaposed with flat steel shapes. Each is a unique sculptural configuration and a complex painterly composition connected to the other Zigs through a shared vocabulary of form and scale. The painted surfaces, individualized with multiple coats of brushed-on automobile enamel, are uniquely imagined for each work. *Zig I* (*page 56*), for example, is treated as a unified pictorial surface independent of its concave and convex planes, while Smith used color to pick out the different forms of *Zig II* (*page 54*), as he had done previously in *Tanktotem X*.

With *Zig III* (1961) (*pages 55, 60, 66*) Smith challenged himself to invent an architectural structure that was not simply a standing relief. His solution was a rectilinear frame with an empty center. Although linked to the two Bouquets, *Zig III* unfolds as a monumental multi-part horizontal structure that incorporates different orders and progressions

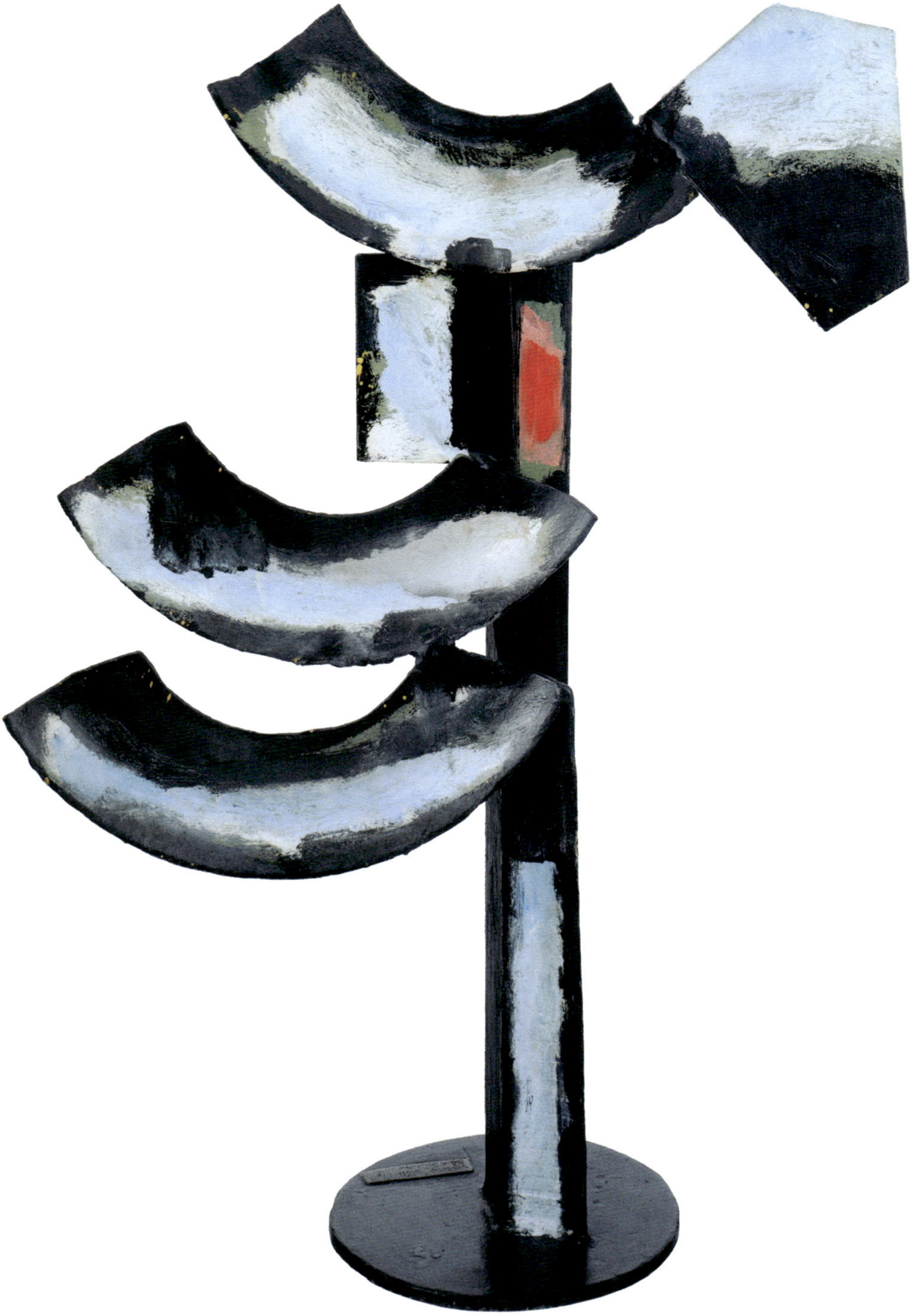

***Black Concaves*, 1960, steel, painted (concave side)**

RIGHT: *Black Concaves*, 1960, steel, painted (convex side)

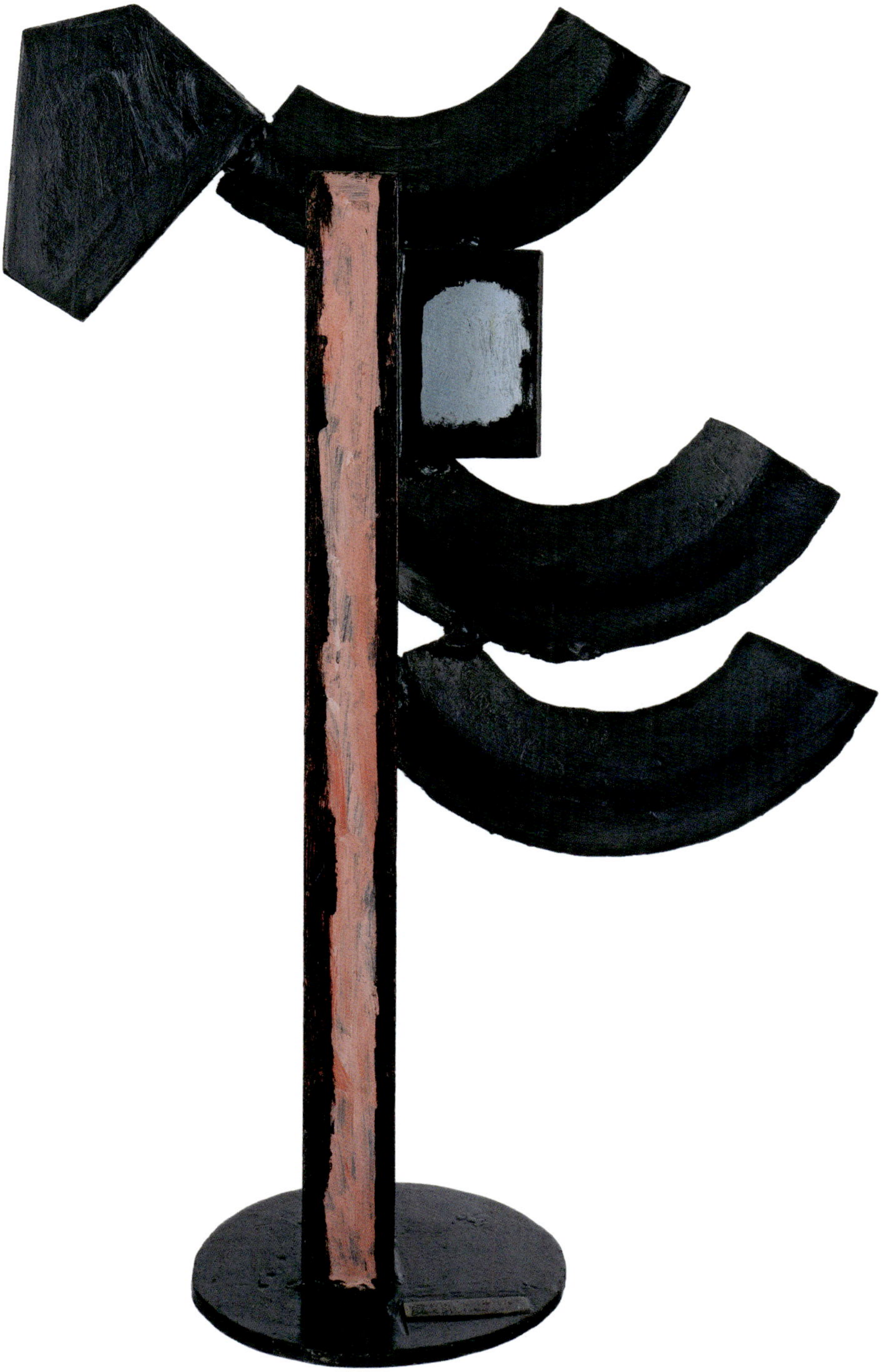

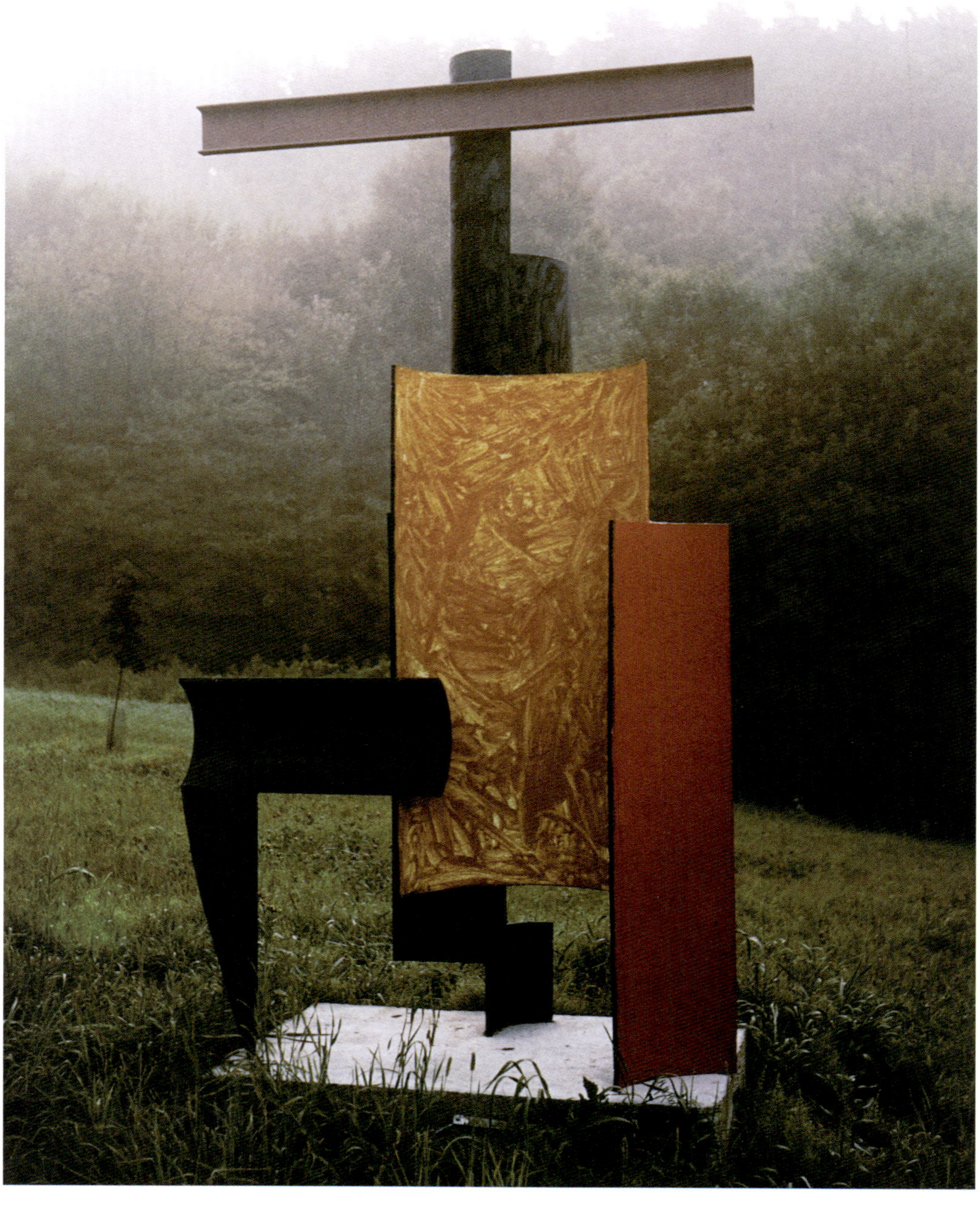

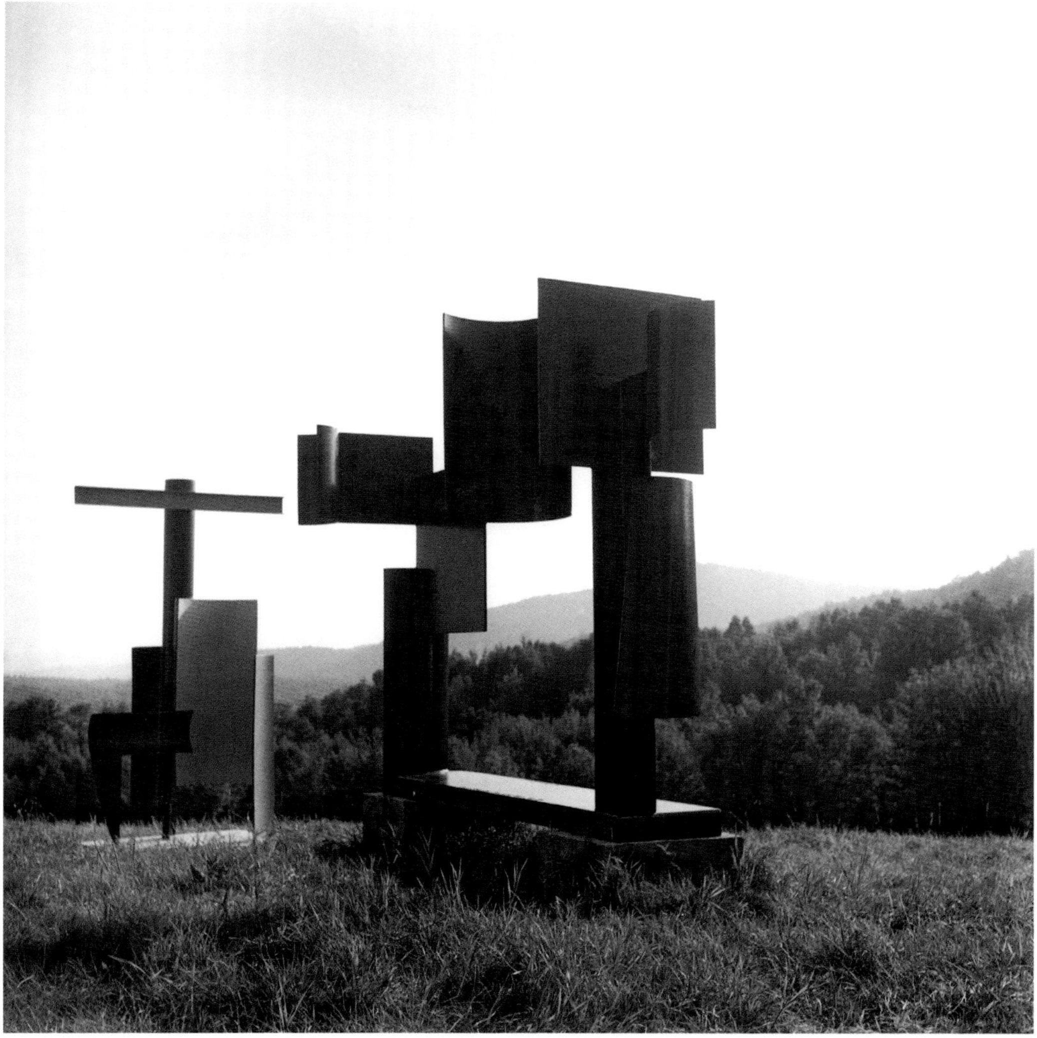

Zig II and *Zig III*, photograph by David Smith, c. 1962–63

LEFT: *Zig II*, 1961, photograph by David Smith

of concave and convex parts in relationships that shift dramatically from different angles. Smith photographed *Zig III* more than most of his other works. One picture, taken when it was dusted with new snow, reveals nature's paintbrush giving added dimension to the blackened sculptural form against the soft contour of the mountains. Smith's chosen camera angle compressed the post-and-lintel structure into a volumetric figure reminiscent of a brush and ink drawing he entitled *Pushup of Concaves* (*page 61*). In the photograph, *Zig III* is transformed

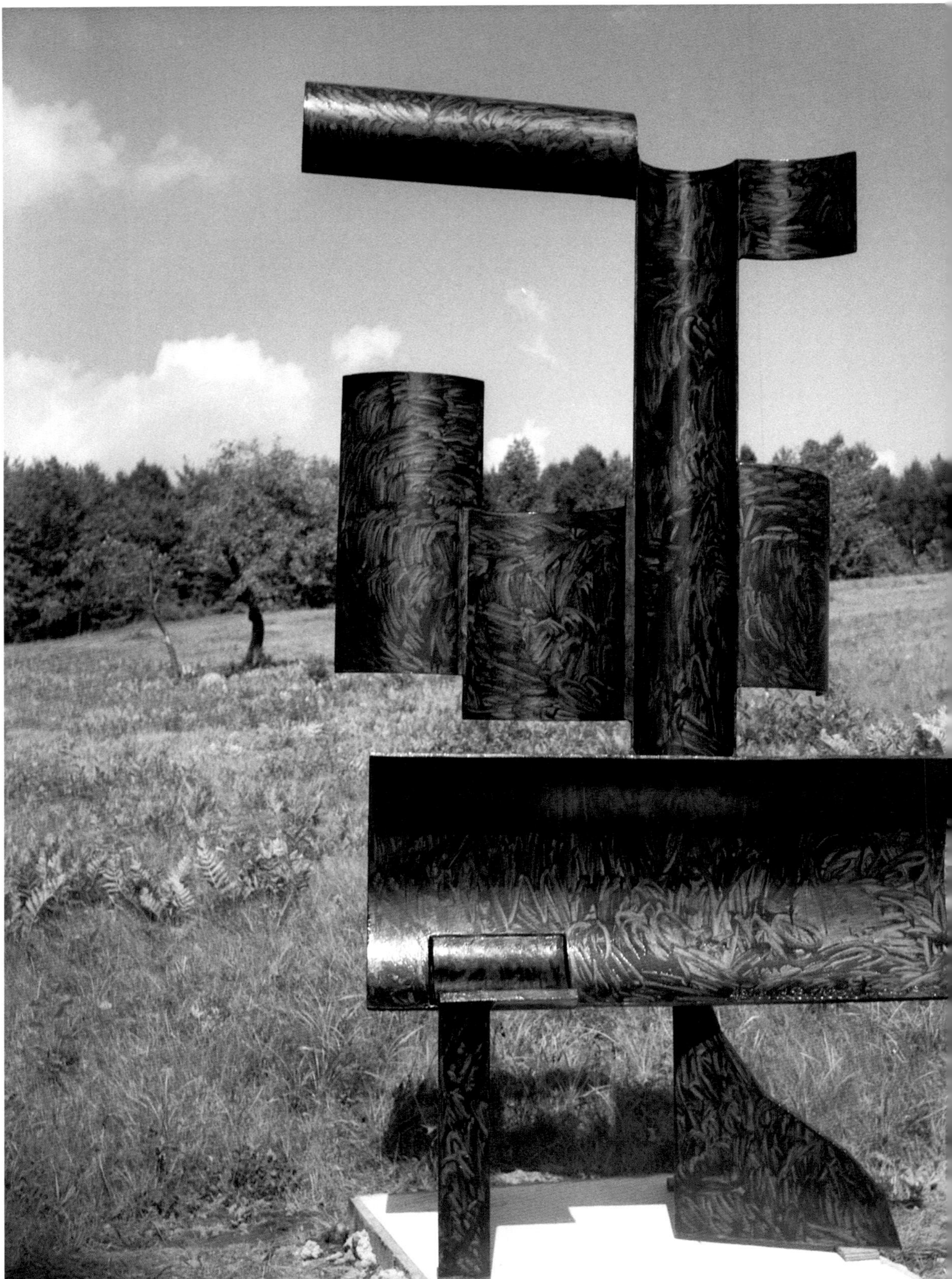

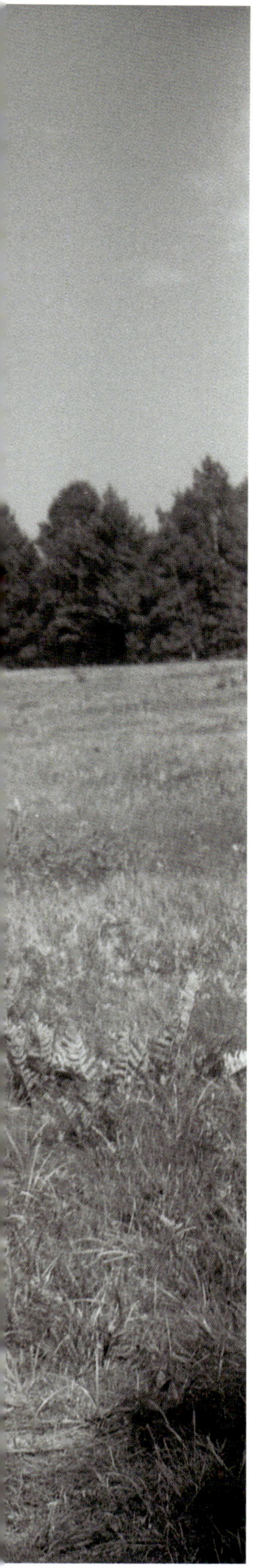

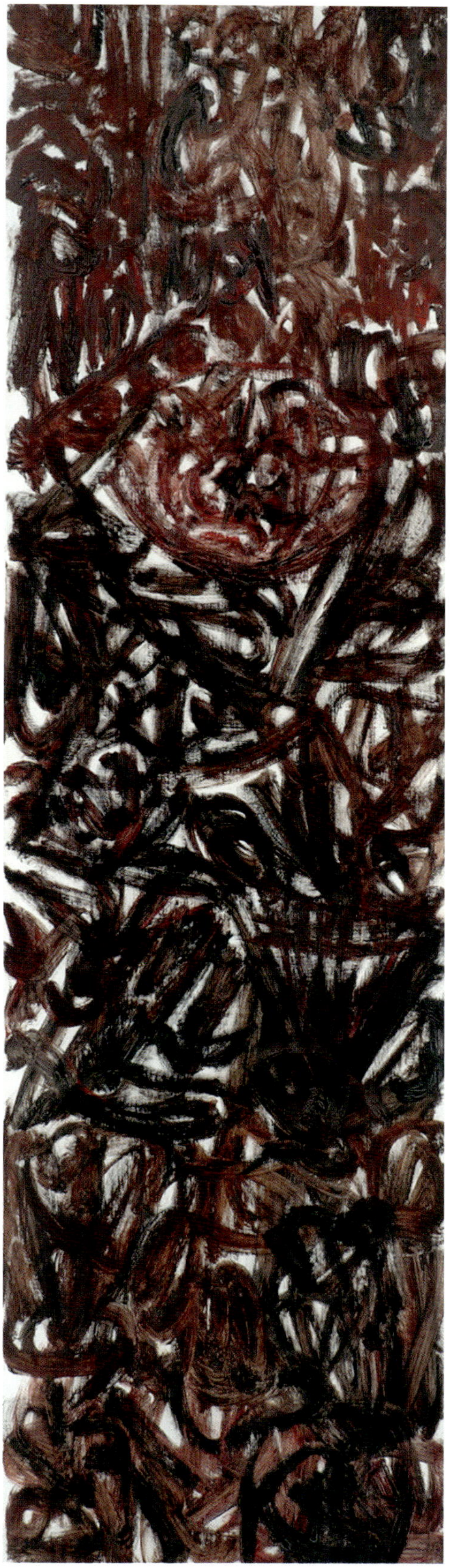

Zig I, 1961, photograph by David Smith

RIGHT: *Untitled*, 1958, oil on canvas

NEXT: *Untitled*, 1957, pencil, oil, and tempera on paper

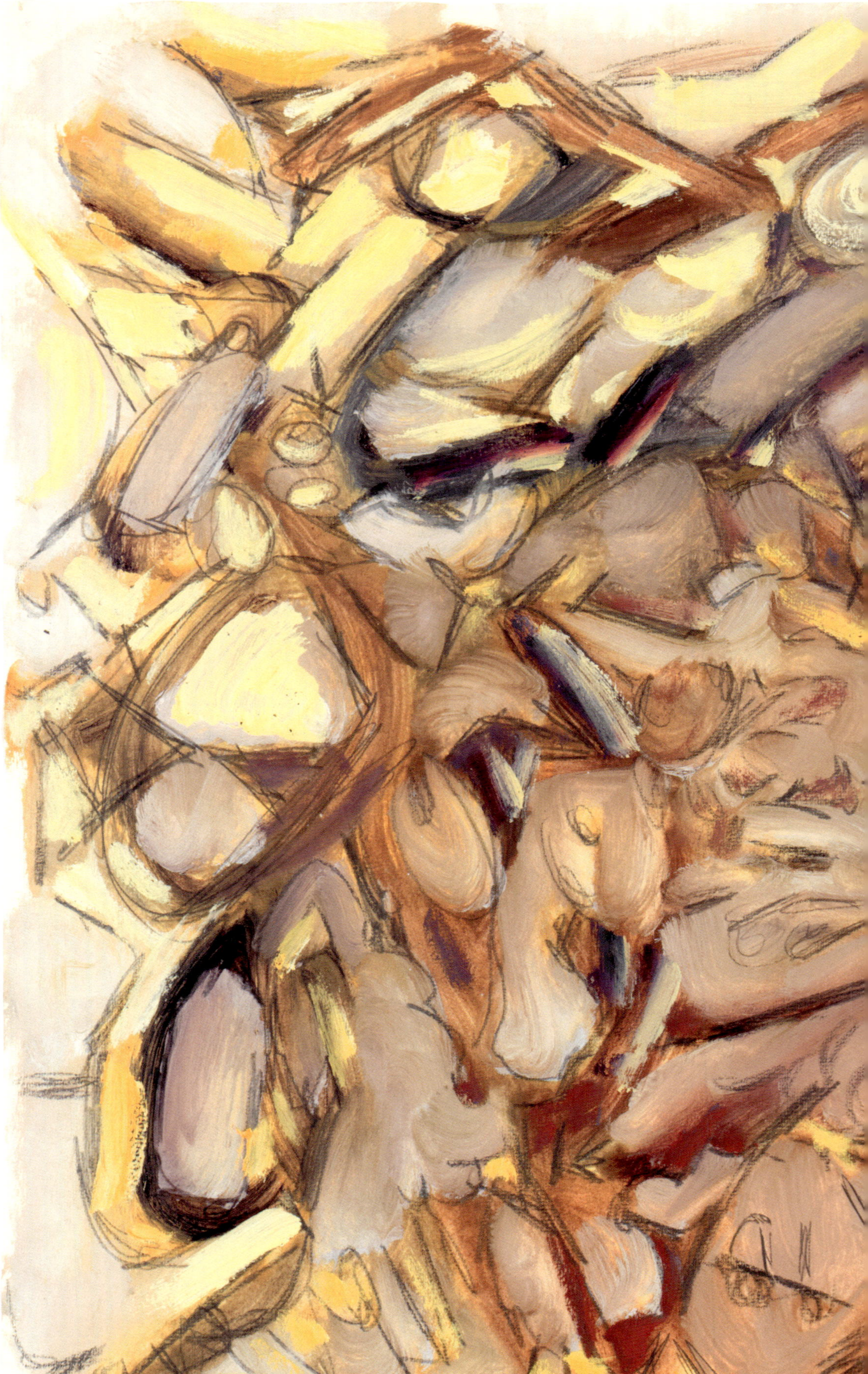

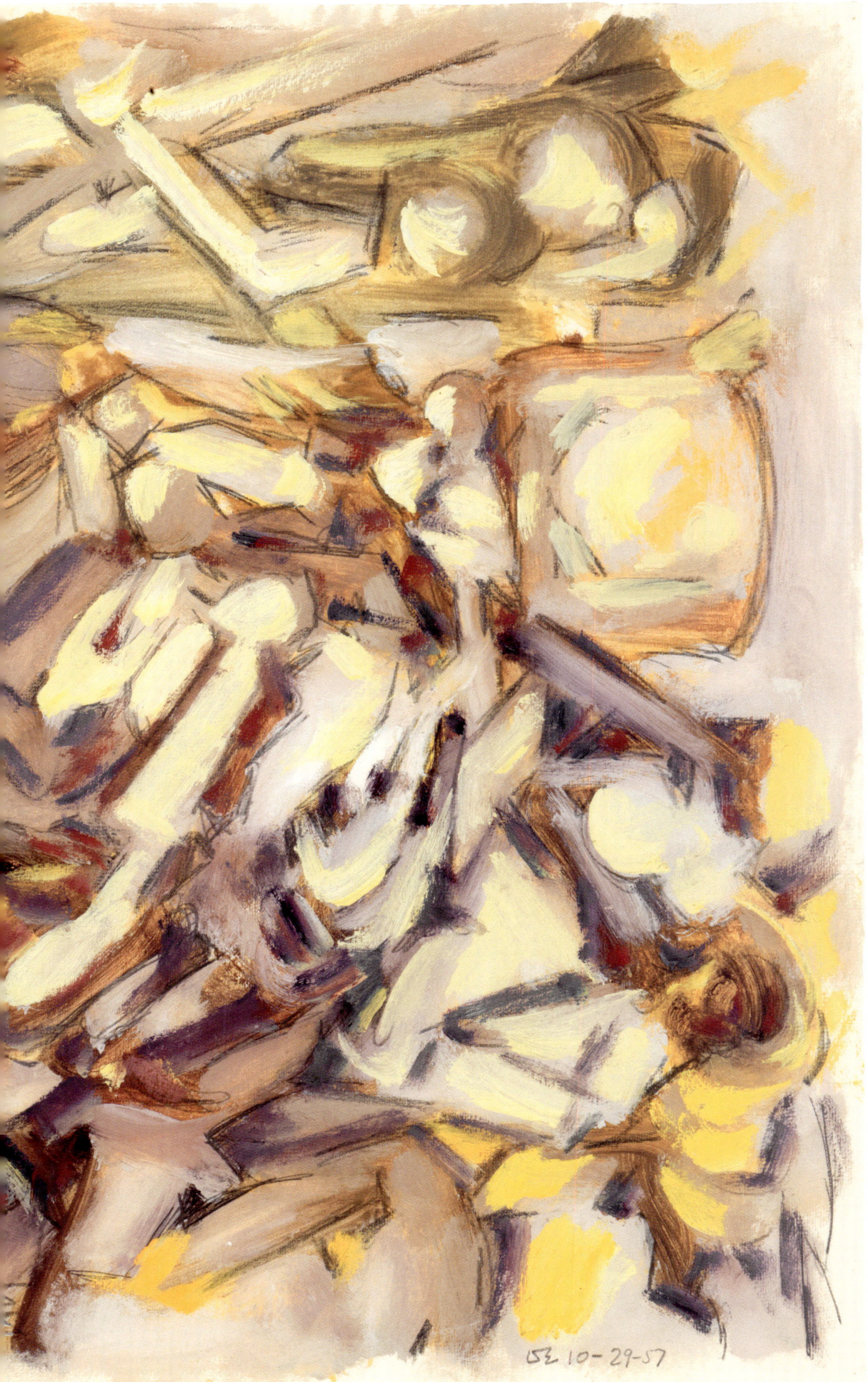
LE 10-29-57

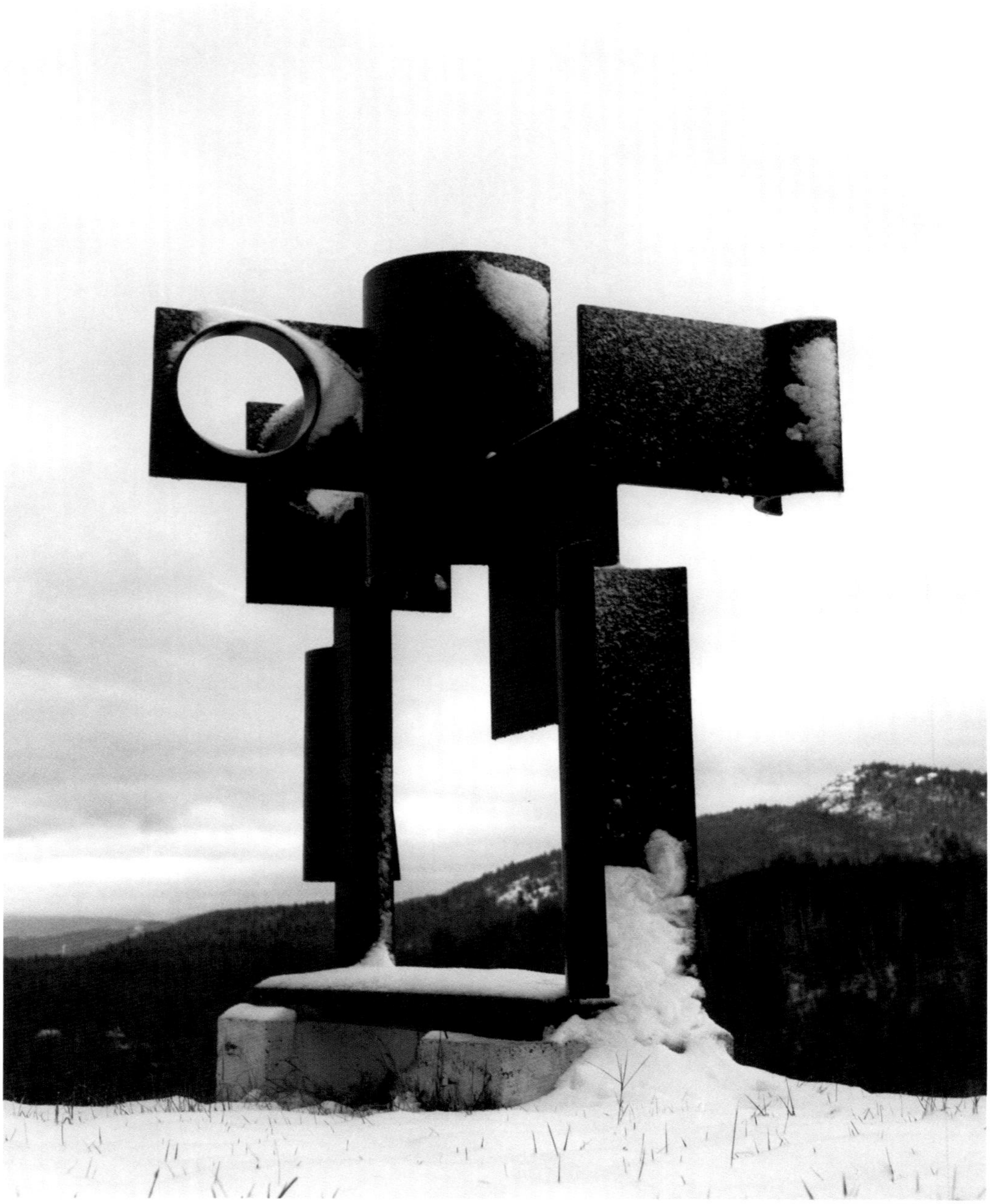

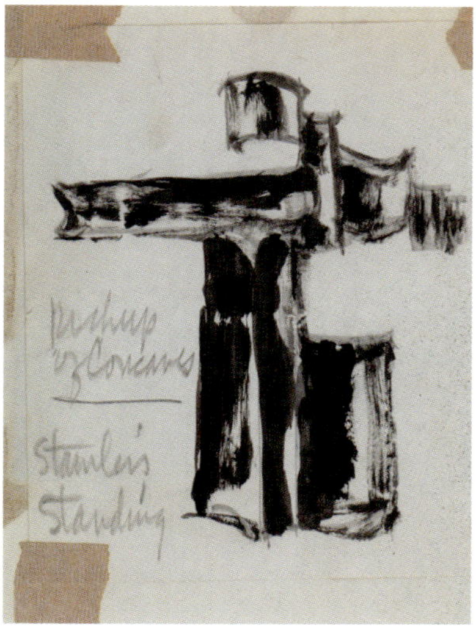

into a towering figure menacing the landscape.

In 1952 Smith wrote of his "realities giving impetus to work that is a train of hooked visions" that can be "recorded, repeated, varied and transformed in analogy."[42] At some point before he died, Smith moved *Bouquet of Concaves II* from the studio to the stone terrace just outside his living room, where it assumed a more active presence.[43] There he could study it and discover its kinship with the other works on the terrace and in the field beyond. When Smith spoke in 1961 about

"realities giving impetus to work that is a train of hooked visions. . .recorded, repeated, varied and transformed in analogy."

the "mystery" of concave and convex, it was in the context of the Tanktotems, but the contrasting forms recur in new variations in some of his later and best works – from the Zigs and *Black White Forward* (1961), to the vertical, stepped structure of *Primo Piano II* (1962) and the monumental tank end that forms the "body" of *Bec-Dida Day* (1963) (*page 12*).

As Smith wrote: "The sculpture-work is a statement of my identity./It is a part of my work stream, related to my past works, the three or four in process, and the work yet to come./In a sense it is never finished./Only the essence is stated, the key presented to the beholder for further travel."[44]

***Pushup of Concaves*, c. 1961, ink on paper, in leather-bound sketchbook**

LEFT: *Zig III*, 1961, photograph by David Smith, c. 1963

NOTES

Epigraph, page 10
David Smith, "The Artist and Nature" in Garnett McCoy, ed., *David Smith* (New York: Praeger, 1973), 119.

1 Michael Brenson, "An American Sculptor," in Carmen Giménez, ed., *David Smith, 1906–1965*, exh. cat. (Valencia: IVAM, Centre Julio González; Madrid: Museo Nacional Centro de Arte Reina Sofía, 1996), 307–08.

2 David Smith to Lois Orswell, July 8, 1959, December 18, 1959, and December 31, 1959, in *Lois Orswell, David Smith and Modern Art*, ed. Marjorie B. Cohn with Sarah B. Kianovsky (Cambridge: Harvard University Art Museums; New Haven: Yale University Press, 2002), 243, 250, 251.

3 "David Smith," in Katharine Kuh, *The Artist's Voice: Talks with Seventeen Modern Artists* (Cambridge, Mass.: Da Capo Press, 2000), 221.

4 David Smith, "The New Sculpture," in McCoy, *David Smith*, 82.

5 David Smith, "What I Believe about the Teaching of Sculpture," in McCoy, *David Smith*, 64.

6 "David Smith," 1961, interview with David Sylvester in McCoy, *David Smith*, 170.

7 "The Secret Letter," 1964, interview with David Smith by Thomas B. Hess, in McCoy, *David Smith*, 175.

8 David Smith, "Notes on My Work," *Arts*, 34, no. 5 (February 1960): 45.

9 Ibid., 44.

10 Ibid., 49.

11 Ibid.

12 "The Secret Letter," in McCoy, *David Smith*, 186.

13 Albert Marshall, "A Study of the Surfaces of David Smith's Sculpture," in *Conservation Research 1995, Studies in the History of Art*, 51, Monograph Series II (Washington, D.C.: National Gallery of Art, 1995), 102.

14 Smith, "The New Sculpture," in McCoy, *David Smith*, 84.

15 David Smith, "Notes for David Smith Makes a Sculpture," in McCoy, *David Smith*, 74.

16 See the insightful discussion about Smith's Sprays in Peter Stevens, "*Sprays:* The Absent Object," in *David Smith: Sprays* (New York: Gagosian Gallery, 2008), 99–103.

17 Ibid., 99.

18 David Smith to Lois Orswell, July 8, 1959, in Cohn and Kianovsky, *Orswell*, 243.

19 The only other photographic record of Smith at work was made by Dan Budnik during visits to Bolton Landing in 1962 and 1963. See Dan Budnik, "David's Steel Goliaths," in *Life* (April 15, 1963):129–33.

20 Invoices for steel delivered to Smith always indicate that all "waste" is to be delivered to him, as well as the requested cut sizes.

21 Paul Hayes Tucker, "Family Matters: David Smith's Series Sculptures" in Carmen Giménez, ed., *David Smith: A Centennial*, exh. cat. (New York: Solomon R. Guggenheim Museum, 2005), 79.

22 David Smith, Smith Papers, III: 0936, notebook 24, c. 1946, as quoted in *David Smith* by Miranda McClintic, exh. cat. (Hirshhorn Museum and Sculpture Garden Collection, Smithsonian Institution, Washington, D.C.,1979), 30, note 2 for "Auburn Queen."

23 I am grateful to Peter Stevens, executive director of the Estate of David Smith, for his insights into this aspect of Smith's working process. Smith often worked in bronze, which allowed him to "collage" together disparate materials and objects that could not be welded together. With this additive process Smith was able to create entirely new objects in bronze. He refused to make multiple castings, arguing that each piece should be unique. He finished the casts himself when they were returned to him from the foundry, believing that the artist must maintain control of the entire process from conception to completion. In a 1961 interview with David Sylvester, Smith stated: "If I make a cast sculpture I make one and all the marks are mine. I don't approve of copies, and I don't make and produce copies...." See McCoy, *David Smith*, 174.

24 Tucker, "Family Matters," 81. Also, David Smith, "The Language is Image," in McCoy, *David Smith*, 79.

25 Tucker, "Family Matters," 81.

26 Smith spent the winter of 1935–36 in Greece and Crete and had books on ancient Greek art in his personal library. At least one Minoan Snake Goddess figurine is in the Archaeological Museum at Heraklion, Crete; another, now disputed, has been owned by the Museum of Fine Arts, Boston, since 1914. These and other examples were widely reproduced in many publications, after their discovery in 1900 at the Palace of Knossos on Crete during excavations by Sir Arthur Evans.

27 David Smith, "Notes," in Cleve Gray, ed., *David Smith by David Smith* (New York: Holt, Rinehart and Winston, 1968), 75. Also David Smith, "Memories to Myself" in McCoy, *David Smith*, 155. The Philadelphia Museum of Art acquired a *Contrast of Forms* (1913) by Fernand Léger in 1950, as part of the Louise and Walter Arensberg Collection. MoMA received one as a gift in 1958.

28 There is almost no tradition of three-dimensional still life in Western art before the twentieth century, and even then, there are very few examples. Picasso's *Glass of Absinthe* (1914), in which the four bronze casts are each painted in an entirely different manner, is the best-known example. Umberto Boccioni's bronze *Development of a Bottle in Space* (1912) is another, but its concerns are primarily with volume and mass in space, rather than with contrasting textures, surfaces, and form. Smith is unique in the postwar period in America for experimenting in sculpture with this traditional painter's genre. See E. A. Carmean, Jr., *David Smith*, exh. cat. (Washington, D.C.: National Gallery of Art, 1982), 158–63, 212–15.

29 David Smith, "Who is the Artist? How Does He Act?," *Everyday Art Quarterly* (winter 1952): 21. Reprinted in *Painted Steel: The Late Work of David Smith* (New York: Gagosian Gallery, 1998), 21.

30 Smith and Motherwell met around 1950 and became especially close after Motherwell married Smith's good friend Helen Frankenthaler, in 1958. Motherwell's Elegies to the Spanish Republic series, begun in 1948, grew to more than one hundred works over the course of nearly forty years. E.A. Carmean notes that, sometime before 1961, Smith encouraged Motherwell to undertake a sculptural version of his painting series, which Motherwell declined to do. See Carmean, *David Smith*, 46–47.

31 David Smith, "Tradition and Identity," in McCoy, *David Smith*, 147.

32 Smith, in Cleve Gray, *David Smith*, 75. Also, Smith, "Memories to Myself," in McCoy, *David Smith*, 155. *Bouquet of Concaves* was included in a solo exhibition of Smith's sculpture at French and Company, New York, in February, 1960, the same month as the *Arts* article appeared. It was sold at that time to a private collector.

33 In his interview with Katharine Kuh, Smith remarked that working in series allowed him to "try to get out all I have to say" about a particular idea. Kuh, *The Artist's Voice*, 224.

34 Ibid.

35 David Smith, "David Smith: Welding Master of Bolton Landing," TV interview with Frank O'Hara, WNDT-TV, 1964. In the interview Smith said of the *Primo Pianos*, "All of the action takes place on the second floor." See also *David Smith: Working Surface, Painting, Sculpture, Drawing, 1932–63* (Duisburg: Stiftung Wilhelm Lehmbruck Museum, Zentrum Internationaler Skulptur; Galerie Gmurzynska; Milan: Silvana Editoriale Spa, 2009), 88.

36 Smith, "Notes on My Work," 44.

37 Frank O'Hara, "The Color of Steel," *Art News*, 60 (December 1961): 69.

38 David Smith to Herman Cherry, May 5, 1958, for example, indicates Smith's a new appreciation for "Barney and his revolution." AAA Reel 1037, F 318. Copy at Estate of David Smith, NYC. David Smith to Lois Orswell, February 16, 1959, mentions that Smith intends to be at the March 10 opening of Newman's show. See Cohn and Kianovsky, *Orswell*, 240.

39 Gray, *David Smith*, 68.

40 Belle Krasne, "A David Smith Profile," *Arts*, no. 26 (April 1, 1952): 13.

41 Joseph T. Ryerson & Son Invoice No. 01-700143 (Jan. 10, 1961) lists "H F Seam Pipe" [High Frequency Straight Seam Welding Pipe] in outside diameters (OD) of 24 and 18 inches and in cut lengths of 4 ft-3"; 3 ft- 3"; 1 ft-11"; and 3 ft- 7"; Invoice No. 01-700144 (Jan. 10, 1961) lists "H F Seam Pipe" in 18" outside diameter in cut lengths of 2 ft-3" and 1 ft-7".

42 McCoy, *David Smith*, 80.

43 Photographs taken at Bolton Landing in winter 1962–63 by Dan Budnik show *Bouquet of Concaves II* in Smith's studio, but a photograph taken by Alexander Liberman in mid-May 1965, weeks before Smith's death, shows the work on the terrace outside the living room.

44 Smith, "Who is the Artist?" in *Painted Steel*, 21.

WHAT SCULPTURE CAN NEVER BE: THE PHOTOGRAPHS OF DAVID SMITH

Sarah Hamill

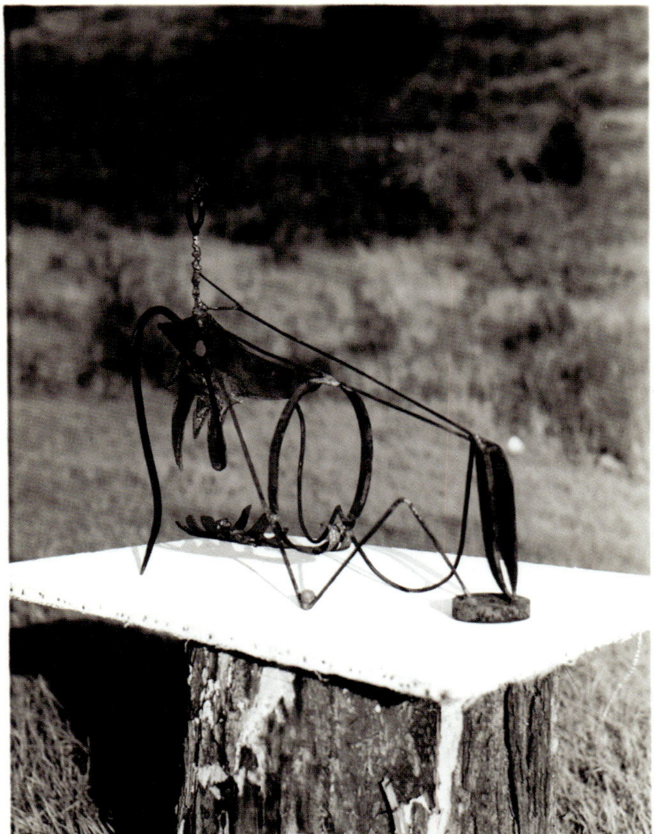

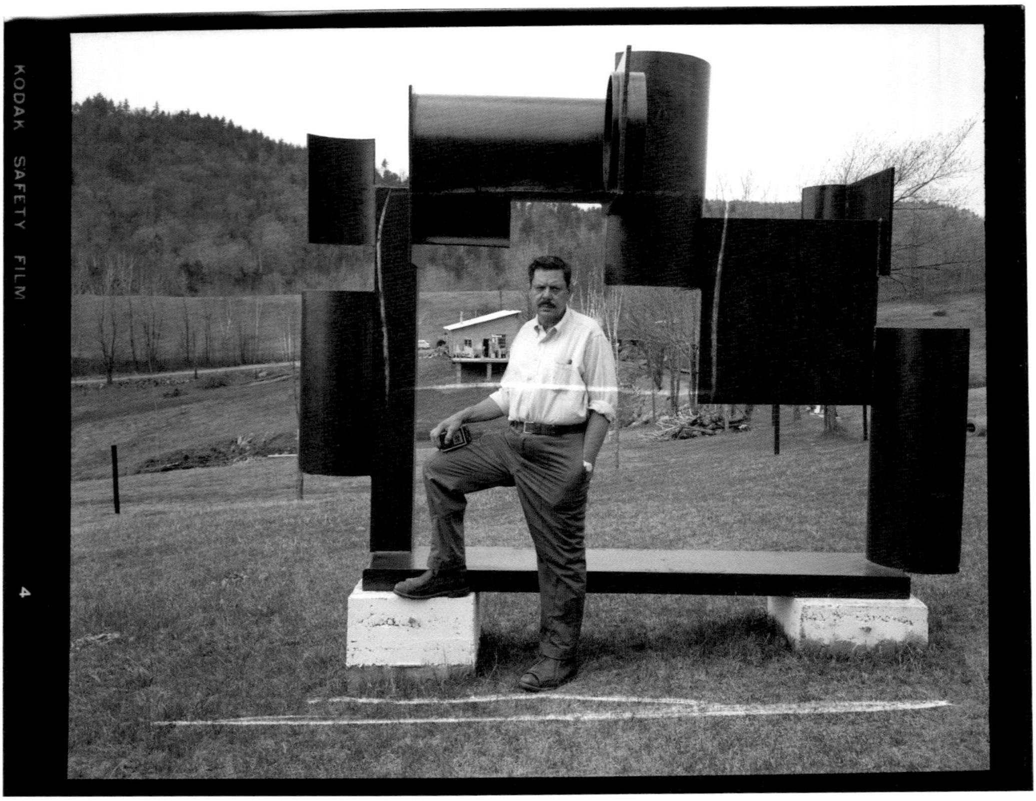

PREVIOUS: ***Suspended Figure*****, 1935, photograph by David Smith, c. 1936**
ABOVE: Self-portrait with *Zig III* at Bolton Landing, c. 1963

When asked to supply a credit line for his photographs, David Smith frequently responded "Copyright TIW," shorthand for the name of his upstate New York studio, Terminal Iron Works.[1] Smith got the name from a Brooklyn welder's workshop, where he made sculptures alongside commercial blacksmiths in the 1930s. After moving to Bolton Landing, he used it as his professional identity when placing orders with suppliers.[2] Its designation in place of a signature for his photographs seems off-key. Official, formal, industrial, the phrase suggests that the artist's photographs be read not as creative artworks – that category Smith reserved for sculptures, his name welded in cursive script onto their supports – but rather as functional tools. Smith's camera, by these lights, was no different from his oxyacetylene torch or steel-toed boots. It was one piece of equipment among many in the sculpture workshop. As a 1961 self-portrait holding a Rolleiflex camera suggests, photography was one aspect of constructing a sculpture (*above*).

In the space of Smith's practice, photography served just such an instrumental role. Beginning in the 1940s, he published his own images in countless journals, exhibition catalogues, and newspapers, launching his steel abstractions into the public realm. A 1946 American Association of University Women exhibition traveled across the Midwest, displaying Smith's photographs in lieu of his difficult-to-transport sculptures. The show persuaded him of the medium's values:[3] "Reproduction seems to act as first acquaintance – and eliminate some of the barriers," Smith wrote to his dealer the next year, registering the power of photographic mediation.[4] So convinced of it was the sculptor that he devoted most of a 1950 Guggenheim Foundation Fellowship to the purchase of photographic equipment.[5] In the ensuing months, Smith reshot his sculptures to date and developed an archival system for the resulting images: each negative was stored in a labeled envelope, a contact print marked with crop lines or other instructions for his printer pasted to its exterior. Smith continued to use this system until his accidental death in 1965. Catalogued, ordered, and archived, the sculptor's photographs were secured as records of his work.[6]

To take Smith at his word – to read his photographs as part of the process of making a sculpture – is to miss the expansive ways in which he deployed photography as an art form in its own right. What are we to make, for instance, of his unsettling – even alienating – staging of sculptures from his *Tanktotem* series on a dock on Lake George? In this set of images, for which Smith brought his recent works down the hill from his studio, the lake serves as a setting for *Tanktotem III*, *Tanktotem IV*, *7/29/53*, and *Bicycle*, which appears, insect-like, in the second picture in the series. Smith's photograph points up his sculptures' figural associations: as figures, the sculptures seem to stand around, their spindly iron legs resting directly on the planks. As objects, however, they seem utterly foreign to their surroundings. In the strange disjunction of abstract steel sculpture and the dock's pastoral setting, the objects appear to both belong to, and remain separate from, their lakeside environment. Such incompatibility animates the work and points up its uniqueness – its particular mode of abstraction, or non-belonging.

If the photographs of the sculptures on the dock use context to point up their abstraction, the low vantage points that Smith used consistently to document single sculptures from the late 1940s onward isolate and dramatize his forms. In a color transparency, *Raven V* is seen aloft, high above the ground, a result of the camera's low position. The sculpture's shapes and lines swing upward from a narrow strip of steel, against a deep blue sky that serves as backdrop for the gleaming metal. Point of view calls attention to the form, highlighting its curving, joining parts. But it also dramatizes sculptural content: *Raven V* is magnified and enlarged through the low vantage point. The "bird" takes on monumental proportions in Smith's photograph, towering above the treetops, a looming, massive form.

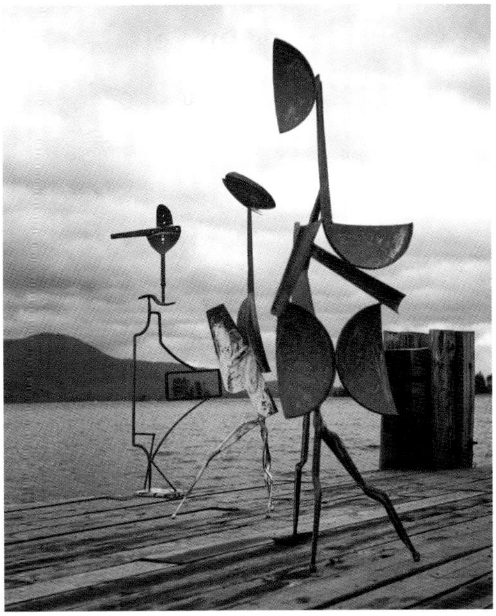

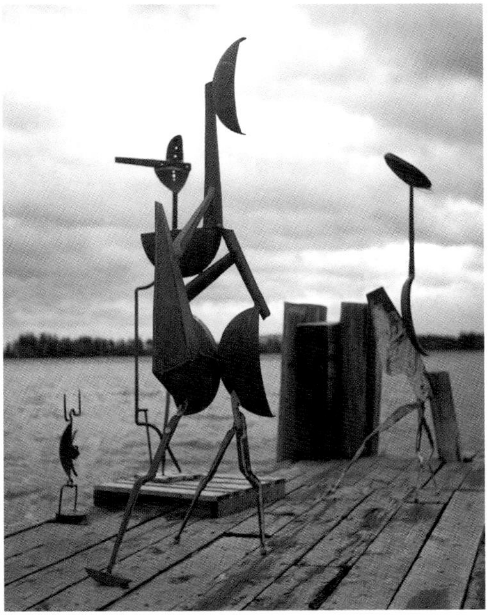

LEFT: *7/29/53, Tanktotem III,* and *Tanktotem IV,* photographed by David Smith against Lake George, on the town dock at Bolton Landing, c. 1953. RIGHT: *Bicycle, 7/29/53, Tanktotem IV,* and *Tanktotem III* photographed by David Smith against Lake George, on the town dock at Bolton Landing, c. 1953

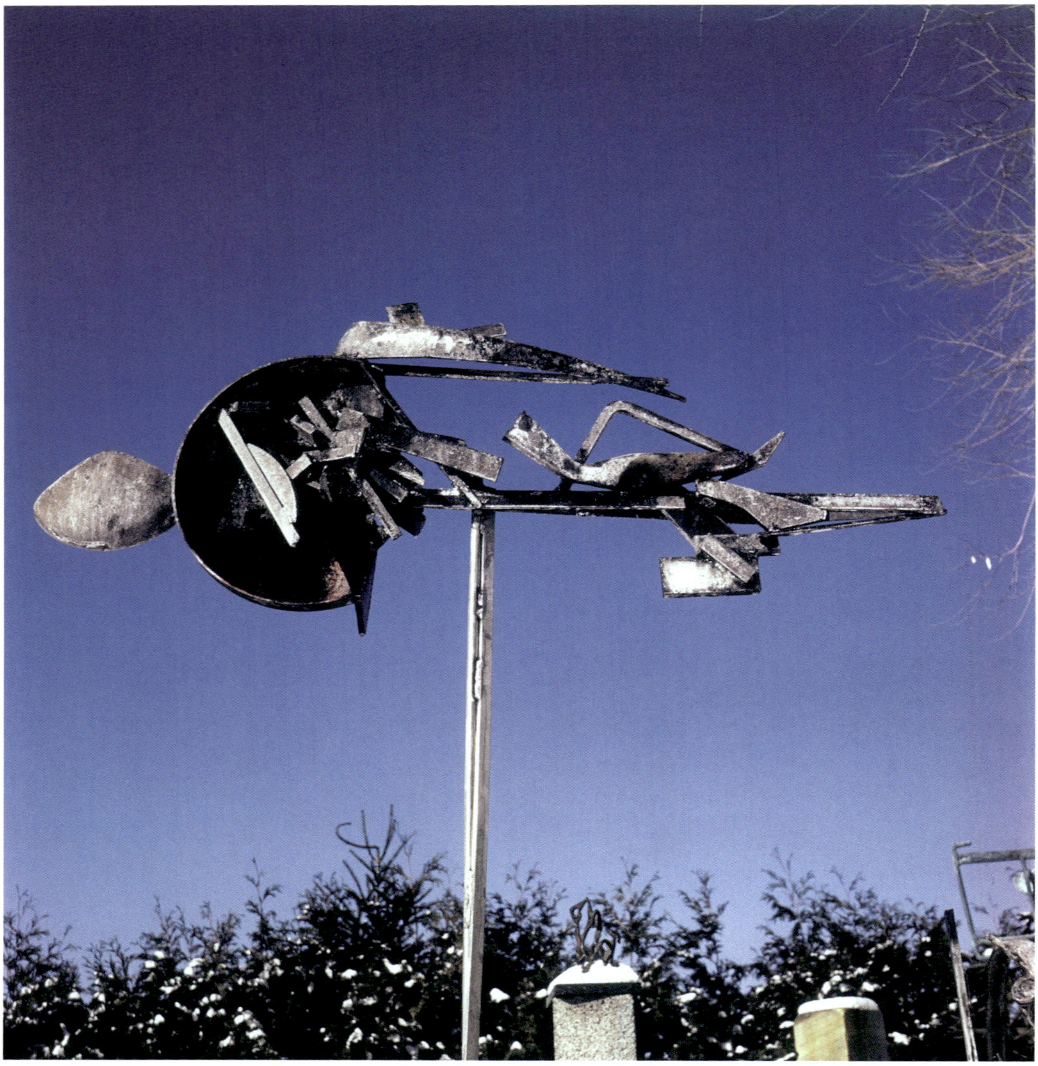

***Raven V*, 1959, photograph by David Smith**

Not transparent records made for an archive or schematic display, these photographs instead reinvent their objects. They supply sculpture with an unconventional setting in the first instance; an unexpected point of view in the second. What results is an image of sculpture that is transformed or remade. Sculpture is envisioned as unfamiliar, separate from the human-scaled world, or it is monumentalized, an object with a scale that appears larger than life. Such views complicate Smith's self-described documentary practices. In his hands, photography was a means to archive and display sculpture, but it was also something else: it was a way to animate a process of viewing, to imagine a visual encounter. Construed in a photograph, Smith's sculpture is imbued with all sorts of expectations and fantasies, meanings and aspirations. It is fictionalized and mythologized in a pictorial framework.

Addressing an audience in Portland, Oregon, in 1953, the artist explained how the medium of drawing operated in his sculptural project. His drawings, he said, represented "sometimes what sculpture is, sometimes what sculpture can never be."[7] They were both a record of his objects and something more amorphous, capable of evoking a set of possibilities – or impossibilities – for sculpture. Smith's photographs echo this dual role, functioning as statement and dream, fact and promise. They reinvent his objects in a two-dimensional framework, calling on photography's claims to likeness to do so.

Since photography's invention, sculpture has been its representational ally. William Henry Fox Talbot's early photographic experiments included numerous shots of the *Bust of Patroclus*, the white plaster cast a stand-in for the human body, which could not withstand the long exposure times of early cameras.[8] Smith, however, joins a group of artists who emerged at the end of the nineteenth century with an altogether different aim in mind: to document their sculptural objects themselves. Medardo Rosso (1858–1928), Pablo Picasso (1881–1973), Constantin Brancusi (1876–1957), and Henry Moore (1898–1986) took the reins of the documentary process from professional photographers, who were often hired by galleries or museums. Each sculptor sought to stage his objects in the public realm, and each used photography as a medium in its own right, sometimes at the expense of the object. Adopting alternative vantage points, unconventional settings, and jarring lighting techniques, they strayed from established conventions of sculptural documentation in their images. In photographs that he printed by hand, Rosso animated his cast wax sculptures by assuming intimate and close-up points of view and by cropping his images tightly.[9] Framed in a narrow view, his sculptures appear as human faces brought to life. Brancusi, in a set of photographs taken in 1923, depicted his sculptures grouped together amidst blocks of stone and wood in the studio and exposed them in a bright flash of light. His images fuse the industrial with the primordial, presenting his objects as a haphazard group. Moore, for his part, used photography to display his sculptures in a pastoral English setting, frequently amplifying their size in a trick of scale. A photograph of *Reclining Figure* taken in 1938 monumentalizes the small form so that it appears on par with the hillside beyond – an image of harmony with nature quite different from the destabilizing encounter with landscape presented in Smith's dock photographs.

These approaches were diverse. And while Smith may or may not have been aware of these particular photographs,[10] they form a wider group of images by sculptors who were committed to the photographic staging of sculpture. In their hands, a photograph was not a straightforward document. It was an independent art form that translated sculpture in a two-dimensional framework. As such, their photographs contain a deeper paradox. At the moment that Smith, Brancusi, Moore, and others were picking up their cameras, they were also redefining sculptural space

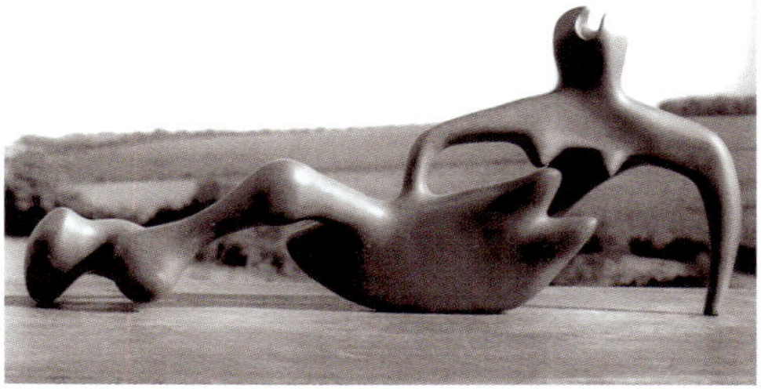

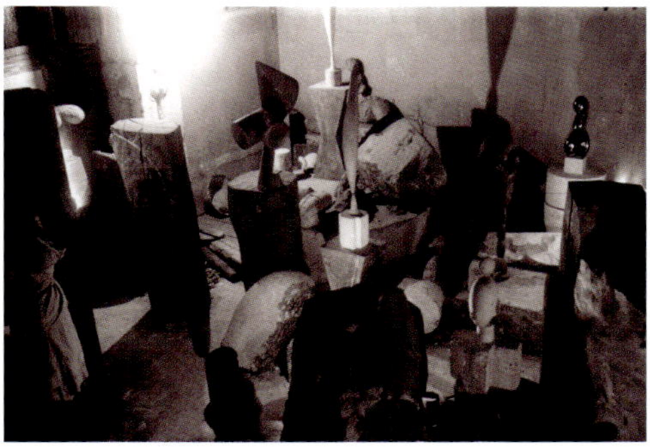

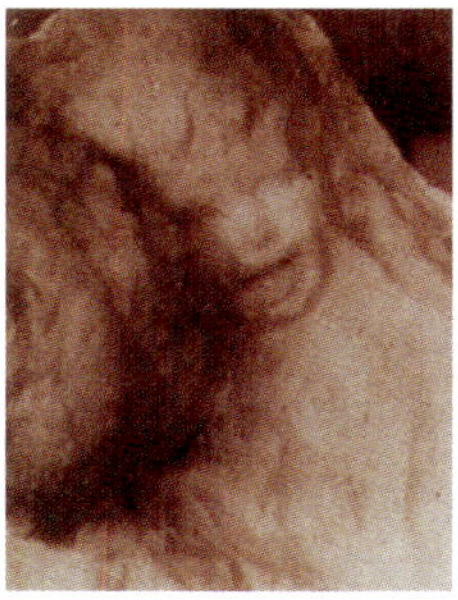

TOP: Henry Moore, photograph of his *Reclining Figure*, c. 1938

MIDDLE: Constantin Brancusi, photograph of his studio, 1923

BOTTOM: Medardo Rosso, photograph of his *Aetas aurea* (Golden Age), 1886–87 (enlarged detail)

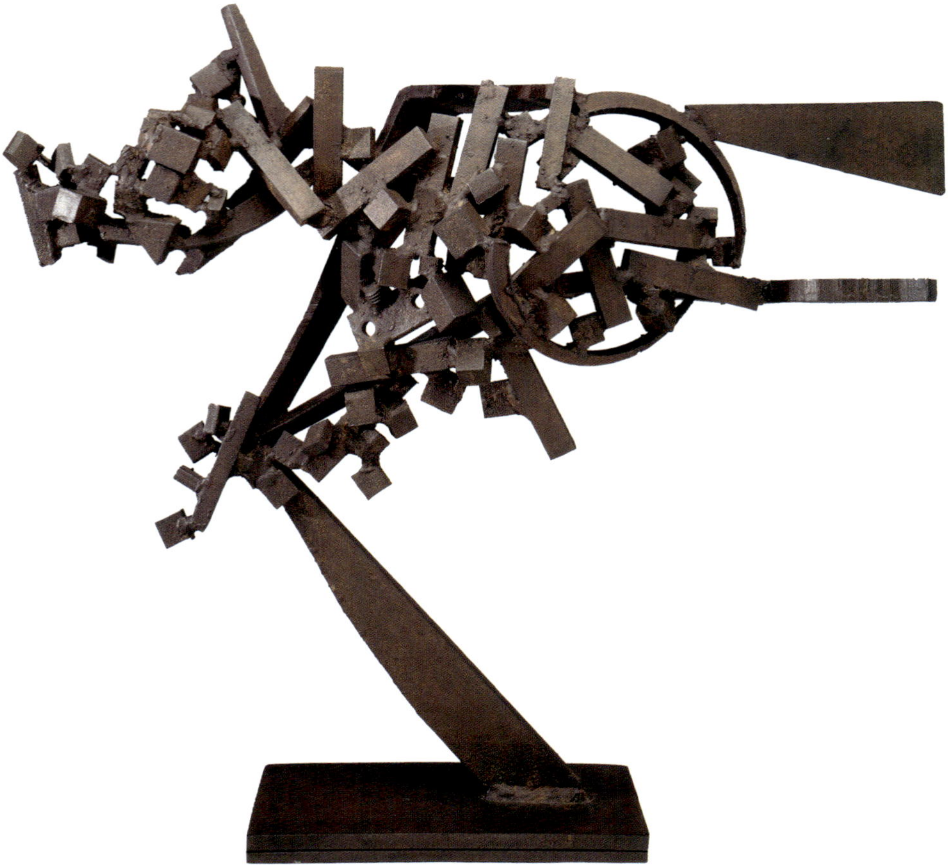

as open and unpredictable. Using disparate sculptural vocabularies, they rejected nineteenth-century legacies of sculptural idealism in which form was synthesized and secured in a stable, pictorial image.[11] These modern sculptors sought to remake the object according to the logic of real space. Or, as Alex Potts put it in *The Sculptural Imagination*, they aimed to "create a new kind of object that would offer a radical alternative to the classicizing and monumentalizing tendencies of traditional sculpture."[12] As photographers, their practices thus raise an important question: why would a modern sculptor committed to spatial and perceptual instability devote himself to photography, a medium that flattened and contained the elusiveness of his sculptural objects? Why risk a return to sculptural idealism, a fixed and perceptually secure sculpture?

The question of space becomes all the more pressing toward the end of the 1950s, when Smith began constructing a new version of sculptural space. He shifted away from linear iterations of form and allusive content – from works like *The Banquet* (1950) or *Hudson River Landscape* (1951), in which pictorial signs or symbols bear abstract meaning, and from works like the Tanktotems and Sentinels, with their linear references to the body. Smith continued to make sculptures in these idioms. But he also experimented with a pared-down version of space – one that Sam Hunter described in 1961 as including "simple, measured relationships" with only "fugitive reminiscences" of the former "loaded, allegorical content."[13] Smith began welding industrial scraps and remnants into open, rhythmic arrangements. In *Raven IV*

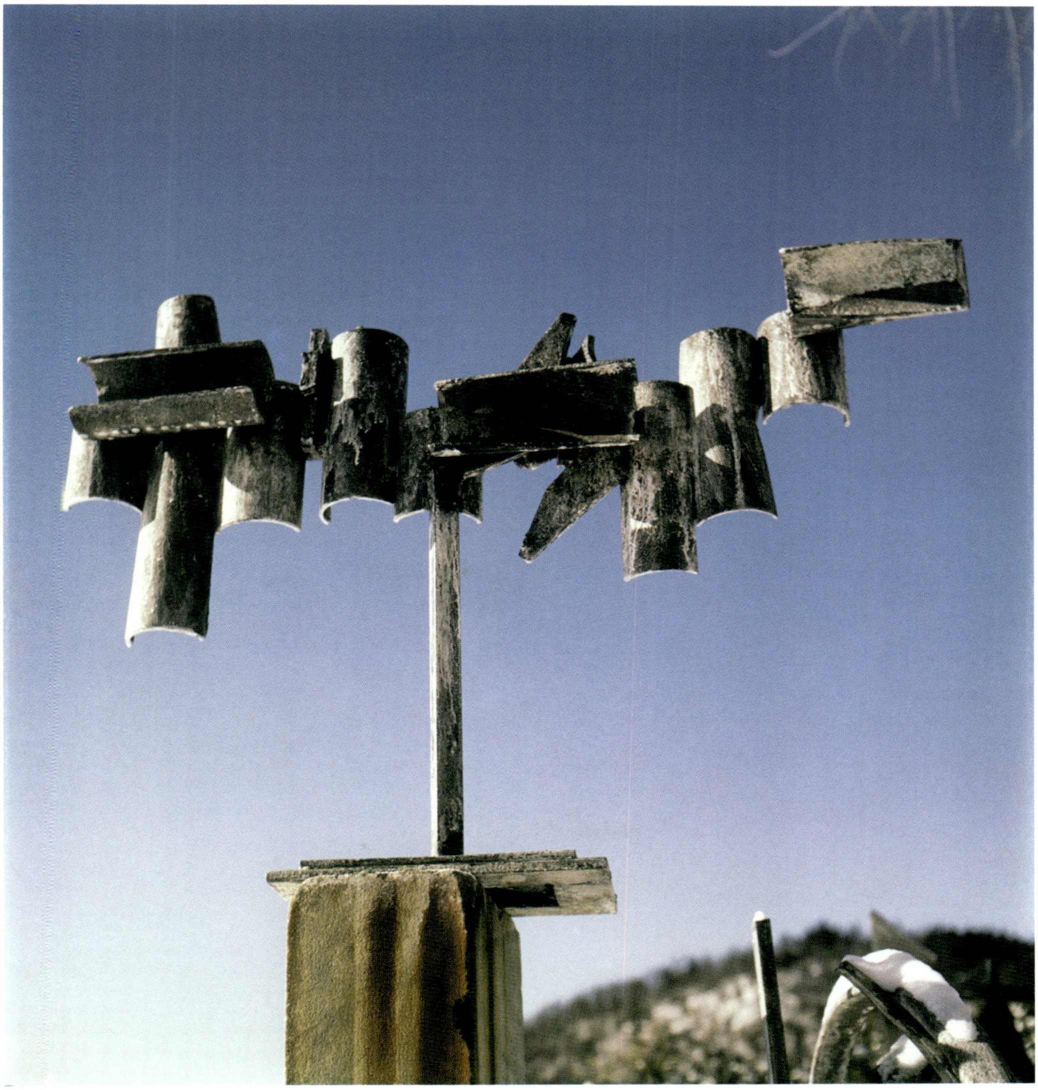

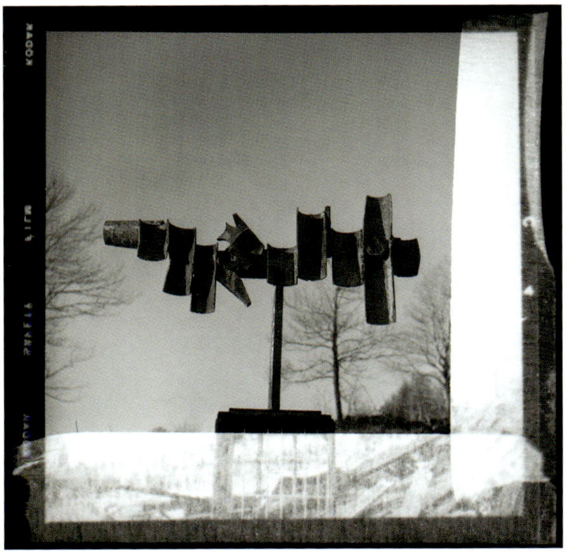

LEFT: *Raven IV*, 1957, steel

ABOVE: *Bouquet of Concaves*, 1959, photograph by David Smith

BELOW: Black and white negative of *Bouquet of Concaves*, 1959, with cropping tape, photograph by David Smith

(1957), for instance, use of irregular bits of steel results in a work composed less of lines than of parts. The experience of viewing the image of a bird is one of moving between open pockets and weighted-down, ragged clusters. In *Bouquet of Concaves* (1959), Smith arranged cut pieces of found industrial parts into a composition – a bouquet – suspended on a narrow bar. The work operates as a melody of open cylinders – each one containing and expressing a different volume. In these sculptures, space is indicated directly, though a set of enclosing forms or open brackets. In the 1960s, in his Zig and Cubi series, Smith built on these innovations, rephrasing his experiments with volume and shaped space on a larger scale.

When Smith turned to photograph sculptures such as these, the problem of space was all the more an issue. How to conjure sculptural volume in a flattened plane? How to translate curving shapes, pockets, and cylinders into two dimensions? Though Smith adopted a range of approaches, he rejected the one that he had used in the 1930s, exemplified in a 1936 shot of *Suspended Figure* (1935) (*page 65*). Most notable about this early image is not its primitive pedestal, a rustic stump. Nor is it the unpainted canvas, an ad-hoc backdrop for the figure's iron form. What stands out – and what Smith subsequently abandoned – is the way in which the photograph grasps the sculpture as a three-dimensional entity. Through its high vantage point and three-quarter view, the image capitalizes on photography's claims to illusionism. The sculpture is photographically and intellectually secured, and little work is required of the viewer to understand how it operates as a three-dimensional unity. Such illusionism was quickly jettisoned in Smith's approach. By the late 1940s, he had developed a photographic language that he would continue to use until his death. It is apparent in his photograph of *Bouquet of Concaves.* The camera is situated well below the object's base, making the sculpture appear to hover high above the ground. (In other images, Smith took this effect to extremes by cropping the photograph at the base of the sculpture.) What is more, *Bouquet of Concaves* is flattened into a plane – one that seems impossible to reconcile with a second view that gives a wholly new appearance to the same sculpture.[14] The

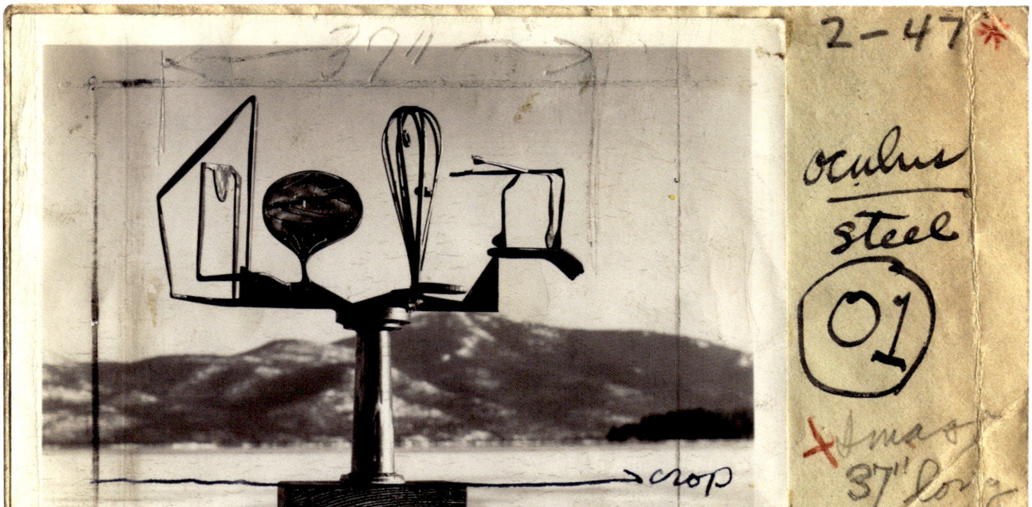

***Oculus*, 1947, with Lake George in the background, photograph by David Smith with cropping marks**

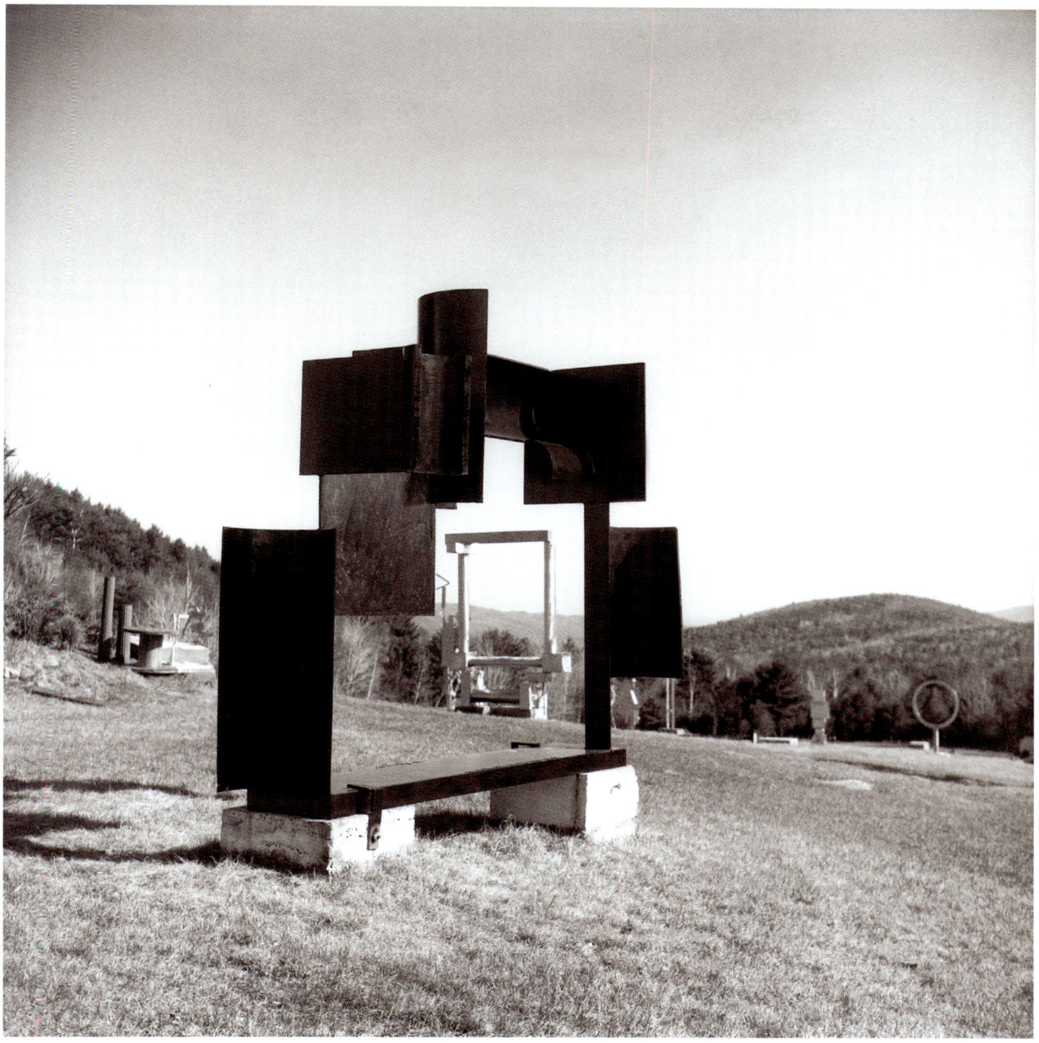

***Zig III* and *Cubi XXIV*, photographed by David Smith, c. 1964**

effect of viewing these photographs is one of disconnection: In addition to being unsure how the two sides cohere into a single object, the arrangement offers no clues to how the work inhabits a ground plane or unfolds into space – information that a shot taken at the sculpture's level, or above it, might otherwise provide. What the photographs do contribute is a pictorial iteration of sculpture. Spatial volume is reinvented as illuminated curves and darkened shadows. The work is pictured as a rhythmic array of light and dark. Rather than representing a sculpture – in all its three-dimensional volume – Smith's photograph presents *Bouquet of Concaves* as it is seen through the mediating structure of the lens. It has translated sculptural space into a pictorial framework.

Smith recognized that his photographs would not replicate the embodied experience of viewing a work in the round. Writing to his dealer, Marian Willard, in 1948, about his photograph of *Oculus* (1947), Smith explained: "The sculpture part takes place at eye level. The photo takes place under eye level."[15] With these simple phrases, Smith named what his photographs sought to achieve: an independent image of his work. By locating his camera low to the ground – "under eye level" – Smith could insist on the

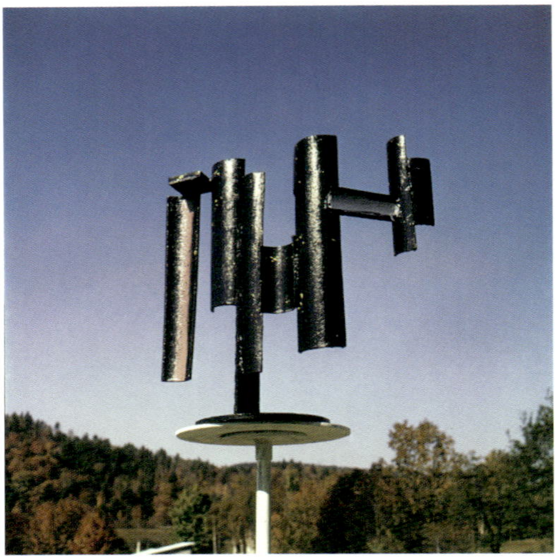

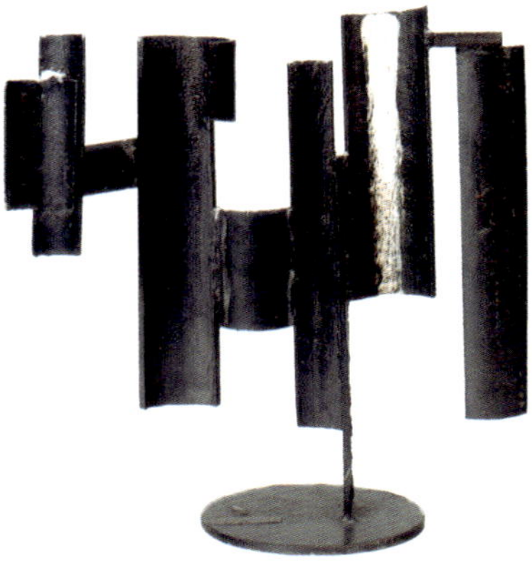

LEFT: *Bouquet of Concaves II*, 1960, photograph by David Smith
RIGHT: *Bouquet of Concaves II*, 1960, steel, painted

mobility of the camera. He could exploit its aperture and frame, translating the sculpture into a flattened plane, as a figure set against a ground.

There were risks in such a pictorial photography, and some of Smith's photographs emphasize the medium of photography at the expense of his sculpture. A view of *Zig III* is a case in point. Here the sculptor has used the camera to set up a play of repeating frames – a pictorial trope anticipated by Smith's dock photograph, in which the rectangle shape of *7/29/53* organizes a distant forested island. The later photograph operates as a pictorial set of nesting dolls: the camera frames *Zig III*, which shapes the chassis-like *Cubi XXIV*. At each step, sculpture and photography collude to point up the camera's composing and ordering mechanisms. In another instance, a composition of *Zig II* and *Zig III* (*page 55*), Smith sought to draw the two works together, imagining them as merging to form an allover cubic structure. The photograph suggests that the two sculptures should be viewed together, as a linked plane.

In other photographs, however, Smith used the medium to shift our perception of his sculpture, as in a photograph of *Bouquet of Concaves II* (1960). The camera has arrested reflected sunlight on *Bouquet of Concave II*'s cylindrical shapes. Lest we think of these highlights as incidental to a hurried snapshot, we should think again. For they are a calculated aspect of the image, clues to the meaning of the work. In the photograph, which has flattened *Bouquet of Concaves II* to a plane, the reflections draw our attention to the sculpture's physical volume. They also draw attention to the pink stripe on the left, a fictive reflection that Smith painted in a concavity, making it appear convex. His inclusion of the real reflections guides a reading of his sculpture, pointing out the complex interplay between painterly illusion, three-dimensional sculpture, and surrounding space.

In Smith's shot of *Bouquet of Concaves II*, as in so many others, a new definition of the sculptor's use of photography emerges. Photography was, in Smith's project, not exclusively a document or record, but an organizing framework for viewing sculpture. It was a way to reinvent his sculptures pictorially. In Smith's full range of photographs, sculpture is imagined as taking part in a human-scaled setting; it is monumentalized as a larger-than-life form, suspended high above the ground; or it is envisioned as a painted canvas, subject to the shifting effects of light. Each of these wide-ranging representations helps to clarify Smith's photographic vision as a process of pictorialization – as a way to isolate, animate, and imagine a visual encounter.

In this way, Smith's photographs open onto a new definition of modern sculpture in which the medium is reliant on photography for its display and its meaning. Seen in Smith's photographs, sculpture is both a tangible, material thing, and a two-dimensional projection in an image. It is both a complexly welded object and its representation in a free-floating image.

Smith's photographs anticipate more recent mixed-media projects by artists such as Thomas Demand, Vik Muniz, Peter Fischli and David Weiss, and Gabriel Orozco. In the hands of these contemporary photographers – or sculptors-turned-photographers – the camera is used to invent an image of sculptural matter or space. In their practices, however, the physical object is often dismantled or jettisoned soon after the shutter clicks. Their projects depart from Smith's in an important way. For Smith, both the sculptural object and the photographic frame were part of the work. As the sculptor emphasized, the two mediums sponsored two separate ways of looking, two independent experiences.

Notes

The author wishes to thank Sue Frank, Susan Cooke, Peter Stevens, and Anne Wagner.

1 To Sam Hunter in an undated note, Smith went even further, writing "All negatives I've sent are mine – I do not want any credit for photos. If such is necessary, in very fine print just say all photos not [otherwise] credited copyright TIW." Manuscript Archives, Estate of David Smith, New York.

2 See Karen Wilkin, *David Smith* (New York: Abbeville Press, 1984), 20.

3 Sarah Hamill, *David Smith in Two Dimensions: Sculpture, Photography, and Space* (Berkeley: University of California Press, forthcoming).

4 David Smith, "Letter to Marian Willard" (January 31, 1947), Willard Gallery Archives, Archives of American Art, Washington, D.C.

5 When applying for a renewal of his Guggenheim grant in 1951, Smith summarized his substantial purchases of a Rolleiflex camera, a 4 x 5 Busch Pressman, and color exposure meter. Smith, "Progress Report on Guggenheim Fellowship, 1950–1951, and Application for Renewal, February 1951" in *David Smith*, ed. Garnett McCoy (New York: Praeger, 1973), 70.

6 Though Smith's photographs were widely published, and Rosalind E. Krauss used them to compile her *The Sculpture of David Smith: A Catalogue Raisonné* (New York: Garland Publishing, 1977), it was not until 1998 that they were sufficiently identified as his own. See Joan Pachner's essays "David Smith's Photographs," in *David Smith: Photographs 1931–1965* (New York: Matthew Marks Gallery, 1998), and "Private Views/Public Images: David Smith's Photographs," in *Sculpture and Photography: Envisioning the Third Dimension*, ed. Geraldine A. Johnson (Cambridge: Cambridge University Press, 1998).

7 Smith, "Untitled Speech, Portland, Oregon" (1953), Manuscript Archives, Estate of David Smith, New York.

8 See Larry J. Schaaf, *The Photographic Art of William Henry Fox Talbot* (Princeton: Princeton University Press, 2000).

9 See Harry Cooper, "Ecce Rosso!" in *Medardo Rosso: Second Impressions* (New Haven: Yale University Press, 2003), 10.

10 Many, however, were published anonymously in journals and catalogues that Smith owned.

11 This model was championed by Adolf von Hildebrand in *Problem der Form in der bildenden Kunst* in 1893, the 1932 translation of which Smith owned. See Adolf von Hildebrand, *The Problem of Form in the Fine Arts*, trans. H. F. Mallgrave and E. Ikonomou, in *Empathy, Form, and Space; Problems in German Aesthetics 1873–1893* (Santa Monica, CA: Getty Center, 1994), 252.

12 Alex Potts, *The Sculptural Imagination: Figurative, Modernist, Minimalist* (New Haven: Yale University Press, 2000), 103.

13 Sam Hunter, "David Smith's New Sculpture," in *David Smith: Recent Sculpture* (New York: Otto Gerson Gallery, 1961), unpaginated.

14 In her *Terminal Iron Works* (1971) and *Passages in Modern Sculpture* (1977), Rosalind E. Krauss analyzed how Smith's sculptures appeared as a series of opposing frontal views, without underscoring the mediation of his photographs. See Rosalind E. Krauss, *Passages in Modern Sculpture* (Cambridge, MA: MIT Press, 1977), 157.

15 David Smith, "Letter to Marian Willard" (February 1948), Manuscript Archives, Estate of David Smith, New York.

UNITY AND IDENTITY: DAVID SMITH'S MATERIALS AND METHODS

Peter Stevens

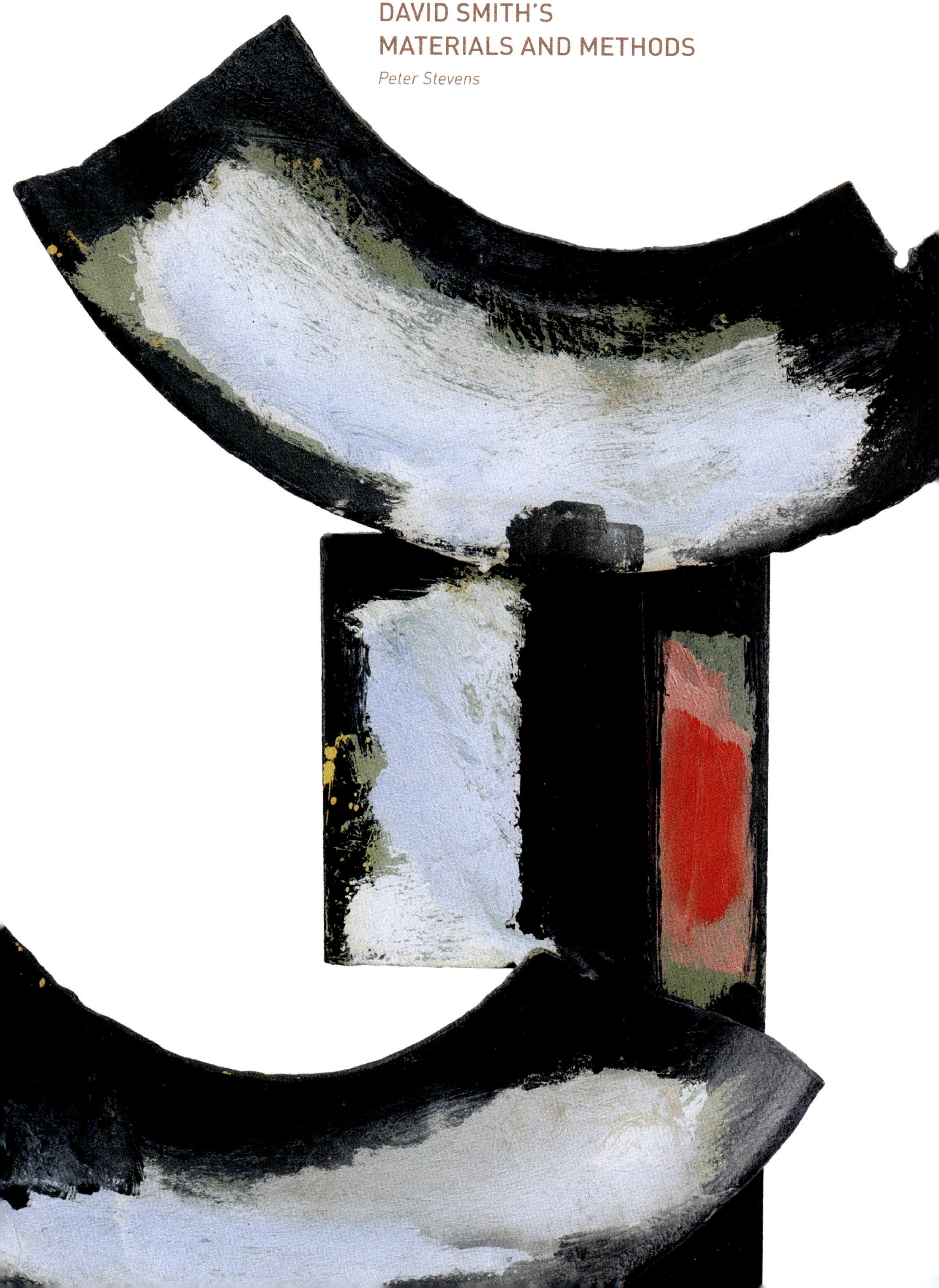

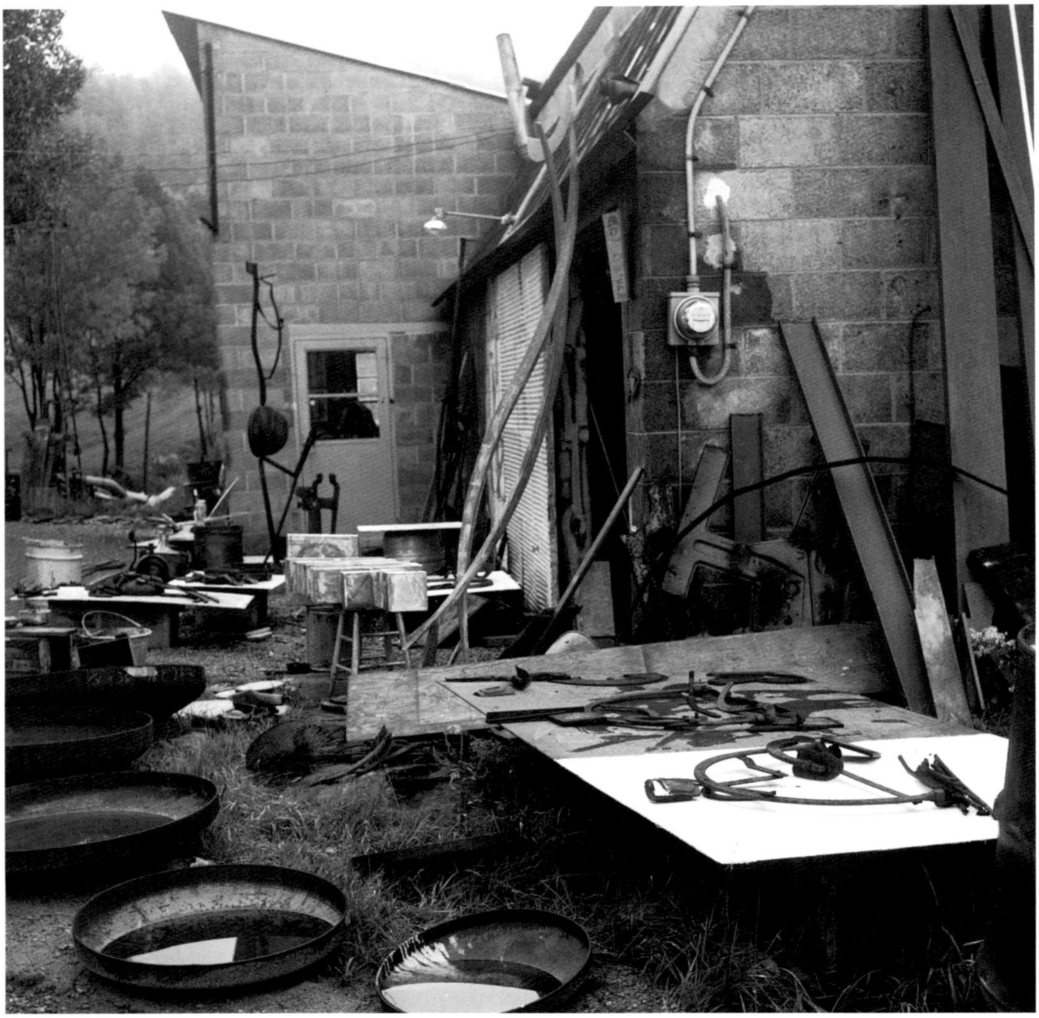

Works in progress outside workshop at Bolton Landing, photograph by David Smith, 1959
PREVIOUS: *Black Concaves*, 1960, steel, painted (detail)

David Smith belonged to a generation thrust into turmoil by the cataclysms of two World Wars and the Great Depression, events that resulted in a world of fragments, dislocated objects, insecure structures, and the threat of chaos. Smith believed that artistic intervention could give new meaning and new identity to abandoned objects by placing them in new contexts within unified wholes. Indeed, unity and identity were central issues for Smith. The concepts informed his unique approach to materials and their meanings, and to the various media and processes that he explored throughout his career. How he defined and developed the two concepts in relation to his work and to himself as an artist sheds light on the broad stylistic and thematic range of his work.

Smith was the first American to make welded steel sculpture. In 1932, the year in which, as a young painter, he first saw welded iron sculpture by Pablo Picasso and Julio González in *Cahiers d'art*, the French art magazine, the entire corpus of welded sculpture, including works by Pablo Gargallo, amounted to a few dozen works. The number of works that Smith could have seen at that time, even in reproduction, was far smaller. He later recalled: "Since I had worked in factories and made parts of automobiles and had worked on telephone lines, I saw a chance to make sculpture in a tradition I was already rooted in."[1]

By "tradition" Smith meant his own personal history, shaped by the industrialization of the rural, American Midwest of his childhood and a no-nonsense work ethic rooted in his strict Methodist upbringing. He was not looking back at an existing artistic tradition when he began making welded steel sculpture in 1933; he was looking forward – to the forging of a personal working method that would incorporate his own experience of a fast changing American culture.

When objects, such as the bits of farm machinery and scrap metal that Smith incorporated into his welded sculpture, are removed from their accepted context, fall out of use, or are simply abandoned, they suffer a loss of meaning. Smith believed that by organizing those disparate elements into a unified whole, through artistic practice, new meaning could be created. It was his conviction that this meaning, manifest in a work of art, becomes a new, shared truth. He referred to the work as a new unity.

The work of art, its source of origin, and its meaning were all conflated by Smith into the single term, identity.

Having absorbed the achievements of the European avant-garde, through his study at the Art Students League with the abstract painter Jan Matulka and mentorship by John Graham, Smith embarked on the construction of an authentic, personal, and distinctly American identity as an artist. As he put it: "Art has tradition, but it is a visual heritage. The artist's language is the memory from sight. Art is made from dreams and visions and things not known and least of all things that can be said. It comes from the inside of who you are, when you face yourself. It is an inner declaration of purpose."[2]

Smith's first attempts at oxyacetylene welding in his apartment in Brooklyn Heights resulted in occasional fires, and in 1934 he moved his work to the Terminal Iron Works,

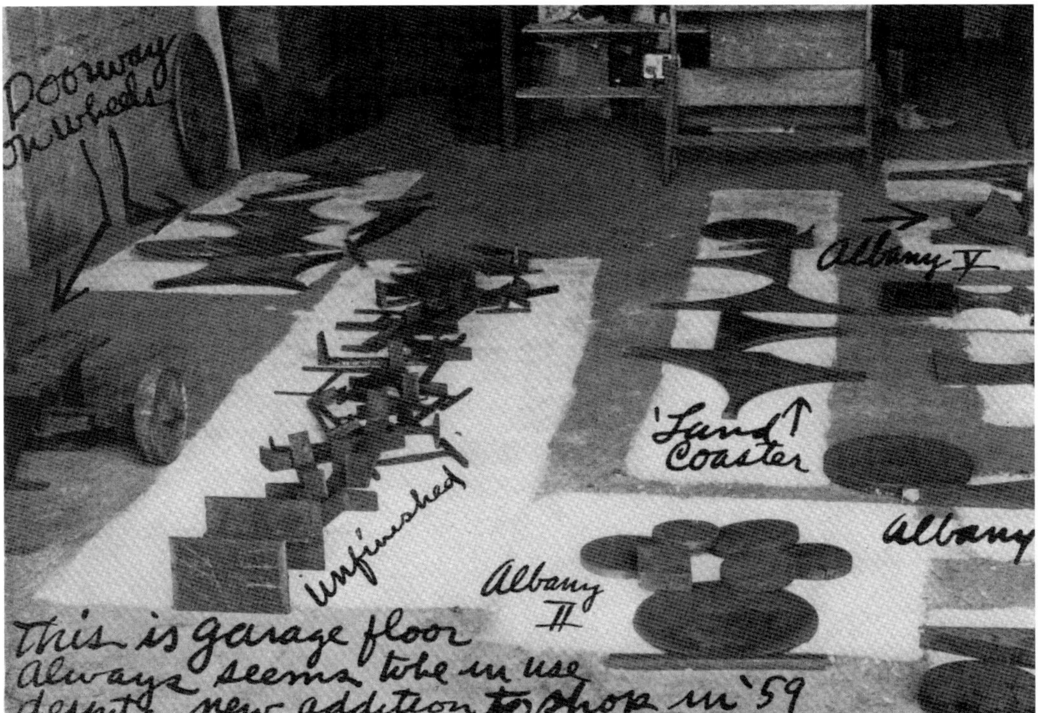

Works in progress on studio floor at Bolton Landing, photograph and annotations by David Smith, published in *Arts*, February 1960 (detail)

a small commercial shop on the Brooklyn waterfront. He began spending summers at Bolton Landing, a hamlet on Lake George, in the Adirondack Mountains of upstate New York. In 1940, Smith and his wife, Dorothy Dehner, moved there permanently. In this remote and rustic setting, Smith united the idea of the artist's atelier, embodied in the studios of Constantin Brancusi (*page 69*) and Alberto Giacometti, with that of the industrial workshop or factory, a site that would later inspire the work of sculptors such as Donald Judd, Richard Serra, and Mark di Suvero. For Smith, the construction of a studio as industrial shop synthesized practicality, politics, and aesthetics, merging industrial methods and the commonplace materials of iron and steel with his highly personal, intellectually and emotionally complex artistic goals. He also refused to accept the sharp divide between the two competing strains of modern art: social realism, with its emphasis on polemical subject matter and storytelling, and pure abstraction, with its claim to a higher universal content. Additionally, Smith rejected the reliance of sculptors on truth-to-materials that had become a standard for carved and modeled work. All of these positions were manifestations of his deep personal need to synthesize unity when

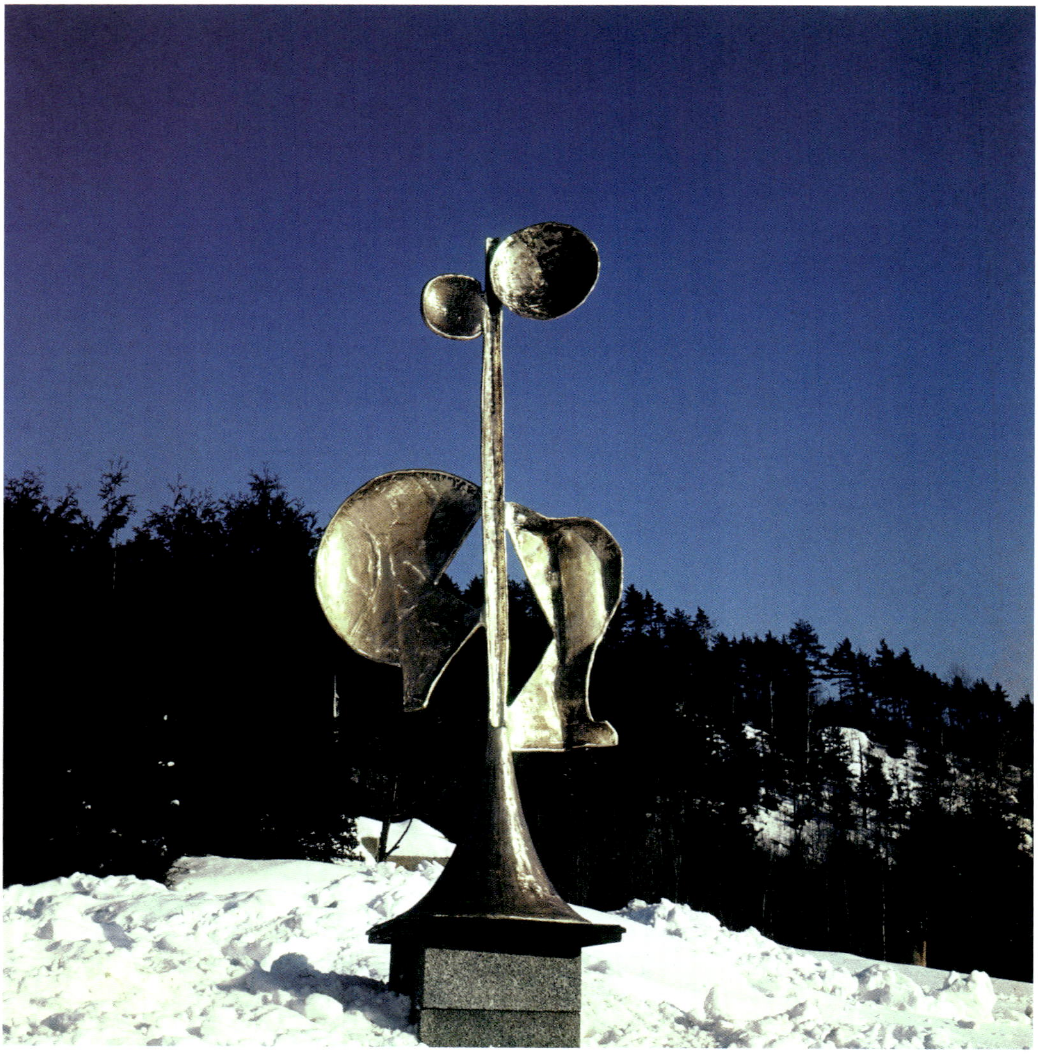

***Auburn Queen*, 1959, photograph by David Smith**

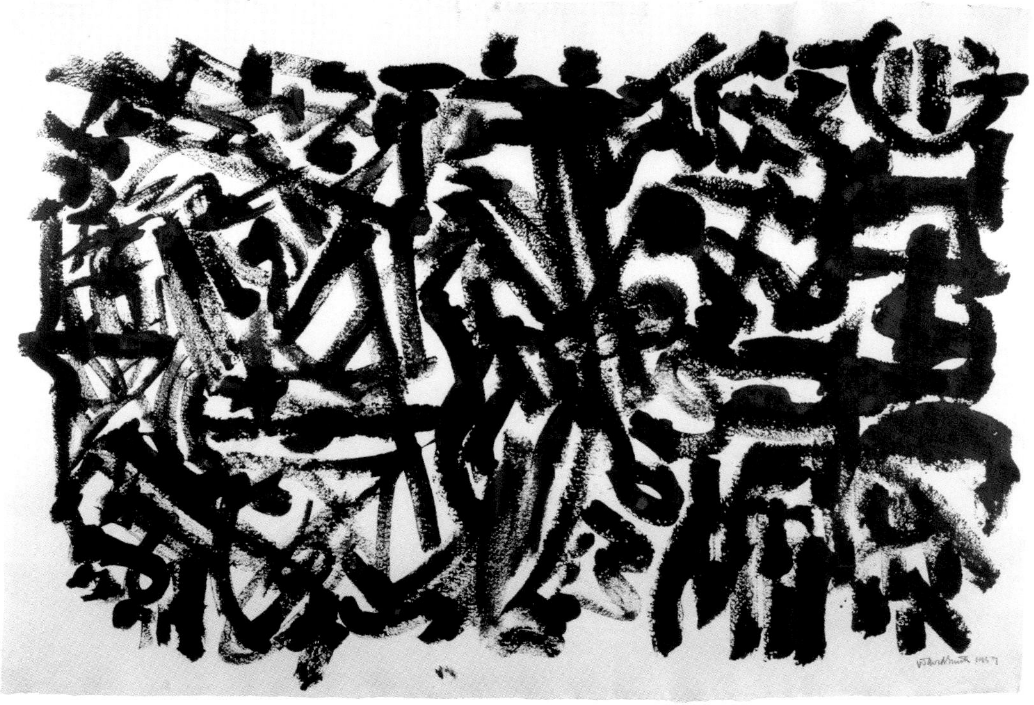

***Untitled*, 1959, black egg ink on paper**

confronted with seemingly conflicting choices. What resulted from this need for inclusiveness was Smith's strong assertion of his unique artistic identity, as well as a working model for a new and distinctly twentieth-century sculptural practice.

Throughout his career, Smith used both oxyacetylene and electric arc welding. When disparate pieces of steel are welded in these ways, the final result is a physically and chemically unified, single piece of metal with a continuous crystalline structure. Whether Smith chose to let the welded joint remain as a visible remnant of the process or to grind and finish it, he was well aware that the resulting construction was literally, as well as metaphorically, a new unity.

Smith did not, however, limit himself to welding, and he did not regard steel (or any material) as neutral. For Smith, materials were freighted with historical resonance. A found machine part, a piece of stock metal, or some unidentifiable object, reworked and translated into bronze by sand casting, were all perceived by him as carriers of meaning that could be transformed through his working process. As he expressed it: "Forms in function are often not appreciated in their context except for their mechanical performance. With time and the passing of their function and a separation of their past, metaphoric changes can take place permitting a new unity, one that is strictly visual."[3]

Smith's belief in the transformational potential of his artistic process is particularly poignant in regard to his use of found objects. His approach differed from that of Picasso and the surrealists, whose works re-contextualized still-identifiable objects. The bicycle seat in Picasso's *Bull's Head* (1943), for example, becomes the bull's head, and the handlebars its horns. The title makes the connection between the found objects and Picasso's vision. The work gains impact because we see "bicycle," but we think, "bull." In Smith's sculptural assemblages, by contrast, his intervention reanimates disparate, unidentified, and unidentifiable objects.

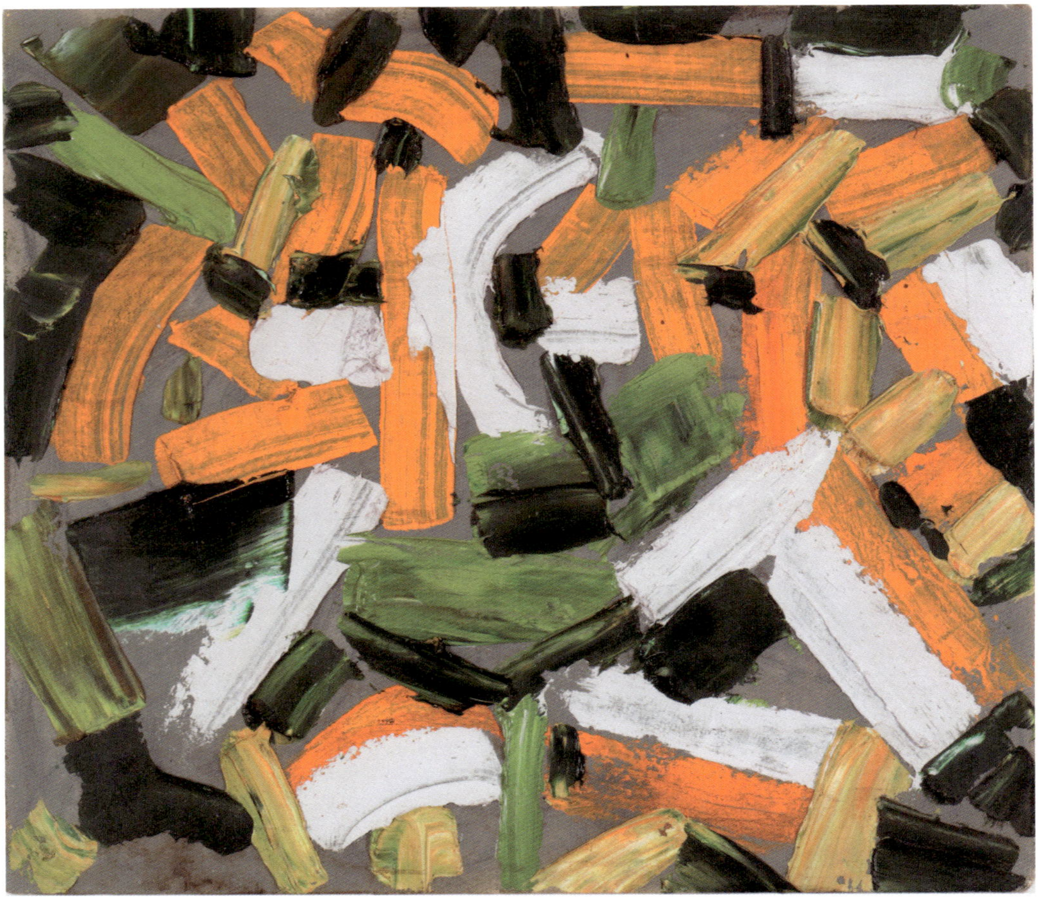

Untitled, **1956, oil on masonite**

Smith believed in the transformation of found objects through the construction of new, unified wholes, canceling an object's status as lost and, by extension, its need to be found, while eliminating the possibility of the kind of word-image linkage exploited by Picasso.

Smith built his personal and artistic identity through the resolution of seeming opposites. He thrived on a refusal to acknowledge boundaries that threatened to limit his vision. He did this through the inclusiveness of his working methods, his materials, and his subject matter. Smith conceived of and constructed his Bolton Landing studio as a metal shop similar to the commercial Terminal Iron Works in Brooklyn. He did not reject the aesthetic solitude of the atelier; instead, he brought industrial methods into it. He did not consider his human industry in conflict with his natural surroundings; instead, he believed it to be an integral and equally valid expression of a larger life force. Similarly, having started his career as a painter, by the mid-1930s, when he began to concentrate on sculpture, he did not turn away from the pictorial nature of painting, or from the potential of drawn line to evoke three-dimensional space; instead, he defined his sculptural practice as encompassing all of these concerns. Smith embraced the historical resonance of bronze and surface treatments such as polychrome paint or traditional patinas. Like the contemporary associations of industrial materials and processes that excited and inspired him, that resonance became another raw material at his disposal. As an end in itself, being avant-garde was of no interest to Smith. He was open to influences as diverse as cubist construction, medieval manuscript illustration, or bird tracks in the snow outside his studio door. He seemed to have no fear of being unoriginal. His openness and apparent need to include and transpose almost every stimulus that entered his life was an essential aspect of his artistic identity, and represented, on a personal level, the unity he aspired to in his work.

The work of making sculpture is relatively slow and arduous. To express himself more spontaneously and directly, Smith turned to drawing, painting, and photography. In his drawings of the 1950s, he used a medium of his own invention: egg ink. Mixing India ink with oily egg yolk produces a medium that reveals the texture of the paper and brush, as well as the speed and duration of the artist's gesture, and gives distinctive detail and depth to the resulting image. The calligraphic gestures in these works and in paintings from the same period resonate with a physical intensity reminiscent of Smith's sculpture. Like his sculpture, many of his drawings are an accumulation of forms. In both the sculptures and the drawings, Smith's process was additive and constructive. Individual brushstrokes in the drawings functioned, for him, like found objects in the sculptures. It was Smith's belief that the transformation of the individual elements of a work, no matter what the medium, into a newly unified whole, emanated from and affirmed his identity as an artist.

Smith's use, almost immediately following its invention in the late 1950s, of industrial aerosol spray enamel to create works on paper and canvas also recapitulates his process of constructing welded sculptures and experiencing them against the backdrop of the sky and fields around his home and studio. The spray medium allowed him to work with found objects – bits of metal, tools, scraps of paper – to create two-dimensional works that

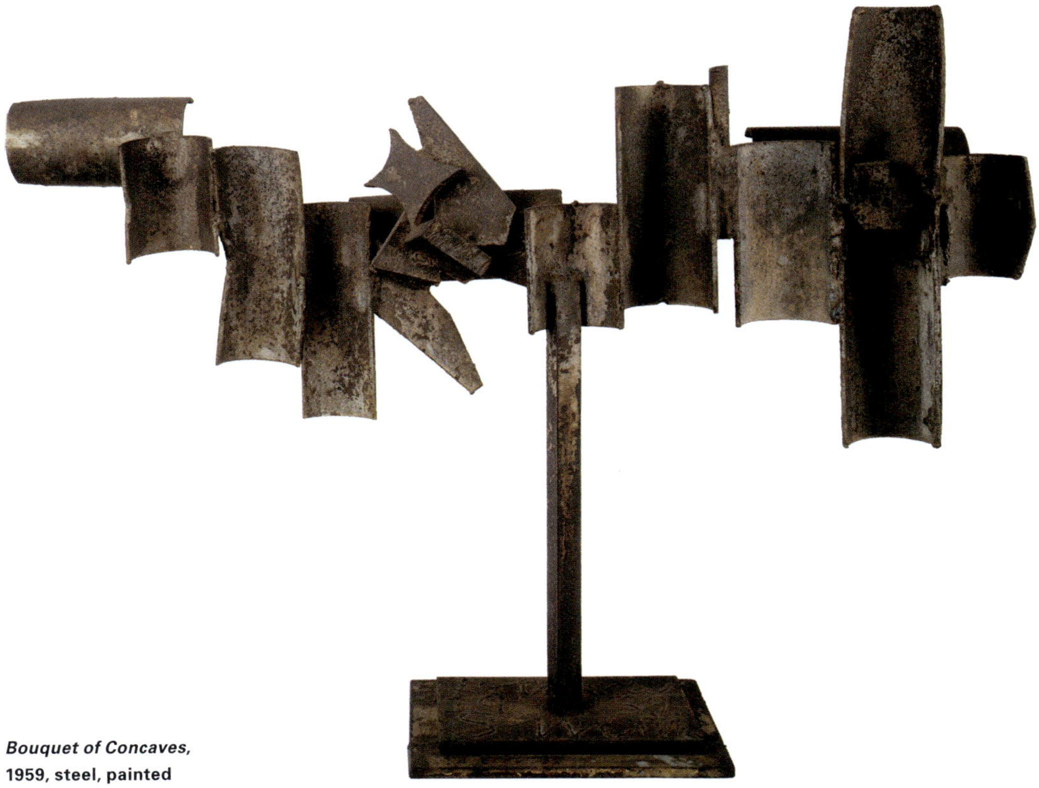

***Bouquet of Concaves*, 1959, steel, painted**

suggest stand-ins for sculptural constructions or constellations unconstrained by gravity. Like egg ink, spray enamel permits virtually instantaneous gestures to record the physical facts of the artist's creative process.

Whether using viscous egg ink brushed with calligraphic certainty across a sheet of paper, rough scraps of discarded steel pipe welded into an abstract bouquet, segments of industrial tank tops unified into totemic expressions of human weight and balance, or industrial enamel paint sprayed on canvases that paradoxically present the absence of objects, Smith treated all his materials as substantive entities deployed in an activated, poetic space. Underlying his work is his belief that all art is experienced as visual image. This had dramatic consequence for his sculpture, freeing him to use any material and, importantly, to consider the surface treatment of each work as a fresh opportunity for aesthetic expression.

On sculptures such as *Bouquet of Concaves* and *Raven V*, both done in 1959, Smith built up layers of acid and paint on the oxidizing metal of the welded forms. The horizontally splayed images that make up these two works are presented to the viewer elevated on vertical supports that rise from relatively small bases. The surface of each work is unified by the patina Smith applied, giving the finished sculptures the appearance of having weathered over a long period. This suggestion of an unknown history gives them a unity and integrity that was essential to Smith's vision. Viewed frontally, these gritty yet delicate works cohere as unified images, each equivalent to a painting or drawing, a reading that is quickly denied as the viewer moves, and their three-dimensionality is revealed. The coexistence of these two distinct realities was a central theme of Smith's work.

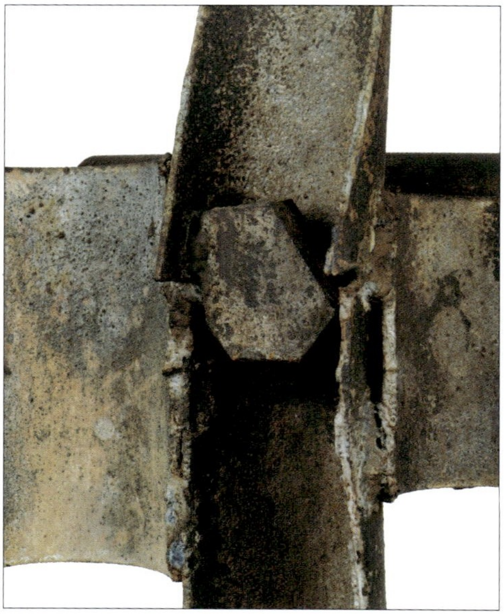

The addition of color, applied in gestural strokes of oil paint, to *Bouquet of Concaves II* and *Black Concaves*, both done in 1960, is further evidence of Smith's expansive approach to sculpture and the resulting challenge he presents to the viewer. The use of paint in these works, as in many of his sculptures of the 1950s and 1960s, manifests the artist's hand and paradoxically asserts both the physicality of the three-dimensional object and its mutability as a pictorial experience.

The diversity of Smith's work resulted from his fecund, creative imagination and drive, and his immense generosity of spirit. It is not possible to discuss here all the media, materials, and processes that he embraced. His works range from pure abstract geometries to sensual figuration. He explored still life and landscape, the generative and destructive forces of nature, and he celebrated the creative power of music and dance. What binds these achievements is their origin in Smith's belief in the moral necessity of the creative act. From the myriad sources, fragments, gestures, bits and pieces of our daily lives, Smith constructed wholes, "unities," in his terminology. His creative act defined his identity. As we view his works, we witness the affirmation of that identity and, by extension, the potential meaning of all constructive human action. That this is in some sense a tautology, an endless circle of blurring artistic cause and effect, may have been the point for Smith.

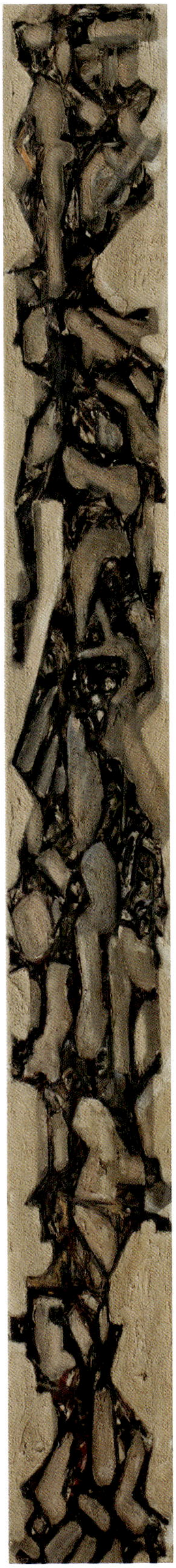

The industrial tank tops that Smith balanced in counterpoint with the lines and planes of the Tanktotems, the accumulated strokes of oil paint or egg ink that he deployed across paper and canvas, the abandoned bits of metal that served as stencils to make his ghostly Sprays, and the scraps of plate and pipe welded into works such as *Bouquet of Concaves*, came to him separated from purpose and isolated from specific meaning. Personal associations and historical resonances inspired him to use each one. As raw materials, all were equally valid to him. Smith called the changes they underwent through his artistic process, "metaphoric." Those changes were, however, also a matter of literal transformation, dependent on the newly constructed objects, the outcomes of Smith's acts of creation. The layered visual metaphors that Smith's works embody express a poetry that resonates in both the physical and the visual experience of the works. Smith believed that his process, originating from his inner being, defined his identity, and offered his work as a shared affirmation of the redemptive power of human action and creativity. In addressing his audience, he wrote, "If you ask why I make sculpture, I must answer that it is my way of life, my balance, and my justification for being. If you ask for whom do I make art, I will say that it is for all who approach it without prejudice."[4]

Notes

1 Cleve Gray, ed., *David Smith by David Smith* (New York: Holt, Rinehart, and Winston, 1968), 25.

2 Garnett McCoy, ed., *David Smith* (New York: Praeger, 1973), 147.

3 Cleve Gray, *David Smith*, 74.

4 Garnett McCoy, *David Smith*, 63.

LEFT: *Bouquet of Concaves*, 1959, steel, painted (detail)

RIGHT: *Untitled*, 1956, oil and sand on canvas

NEXT: David Smith in his studio at Bolton Landing, photograph by Dan Budnik, winter 1962–63

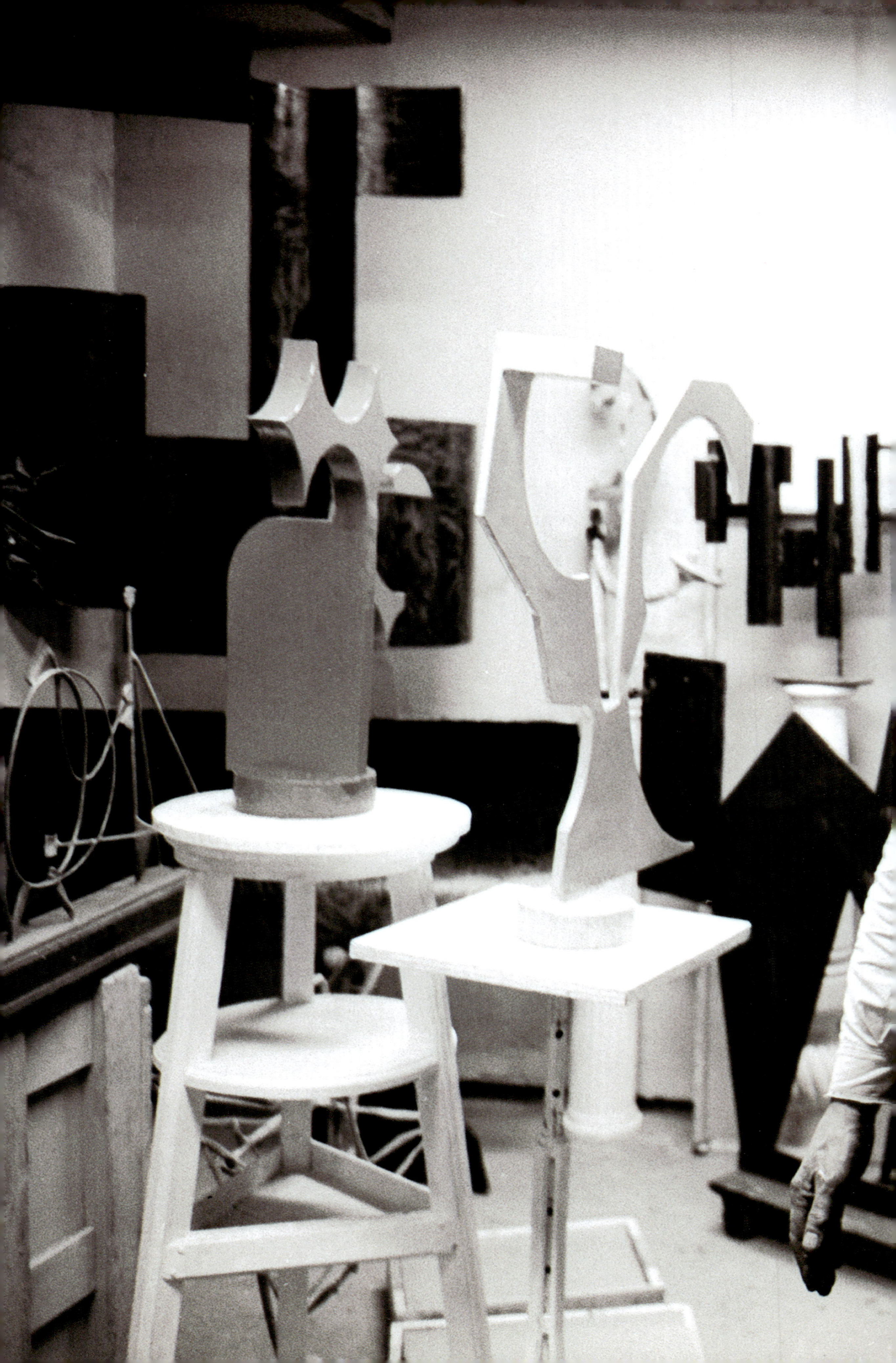

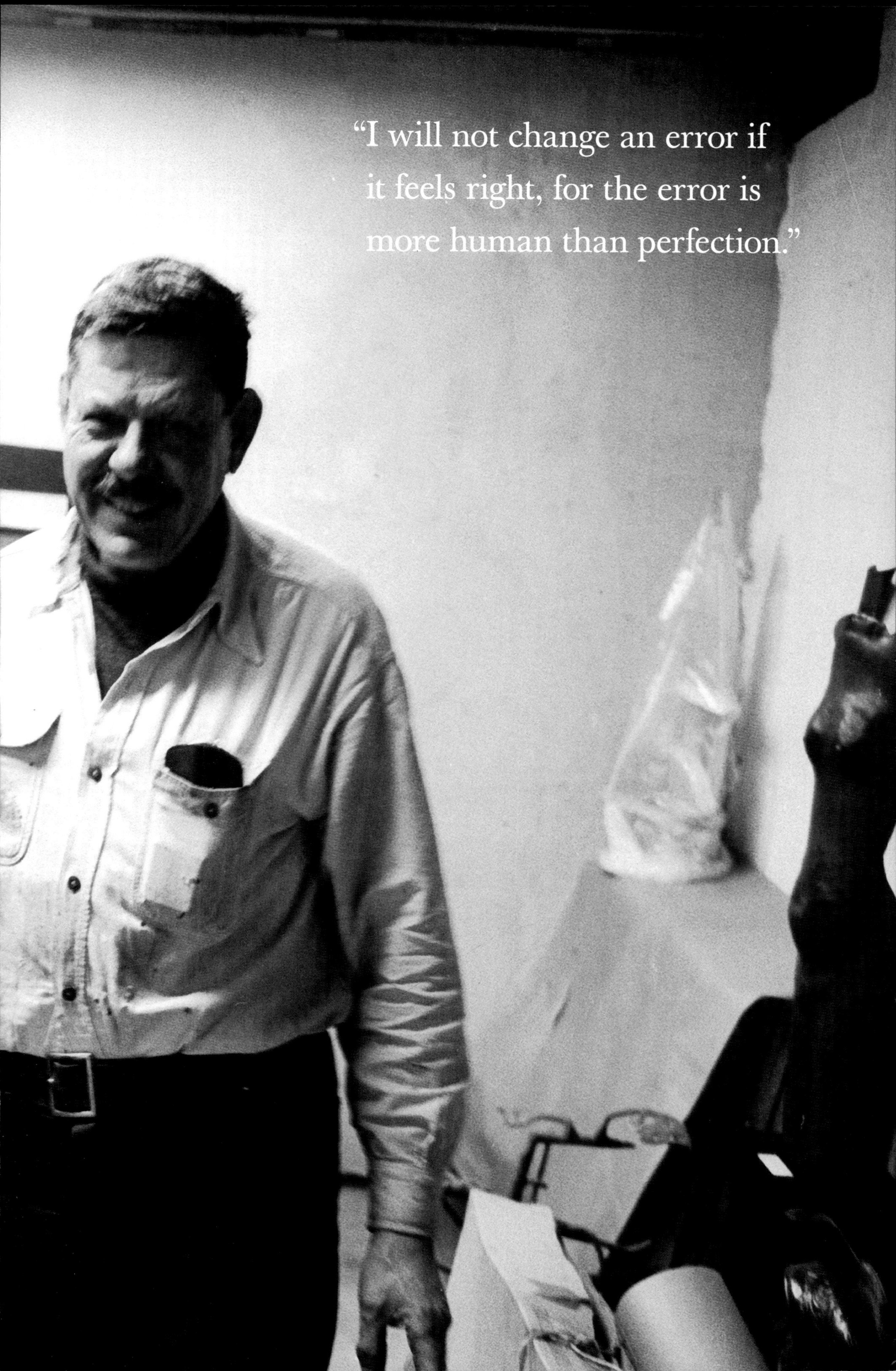
"I will not change an error if it feels right, for the error is more human than perfection."

ILLUSTRATIONS

Works by David Smith

Sculpture

Tanktotem IV, 1953
Steel
92 3/4 x 29 x 35 in.
Collection Albright-Knox Art Gallery, Buffalo, New York. Gift of Seymour H. Knox, Jr., 1957
Page 1

Tanktotem VI, 1957
Steel, painted
103 7/8 x 21 x 11 1/4 in.
Estate of David Smith, New York
Page 36

Raven IV, 1957
Steel
28 1/8 x 32 3/8 x 13 1/4 in.
Hirshhorn Museum and Sculpture Garden, Smithsonian Institution, Gift of Joseph H. Hirshhorn, 1966
Page 70

Raven V, 1959
Steel
59 x 55 x 11 in.
Storm King Art Center, Mountainville, New York, Gift of the Ralph E. Ogden Foundation, Inc.
Page 42

Auburn Queen, 1959
Bronze
86 3/8 x 36 3/4 x 21 5/8 in.
Hirshhorn Museum and Sculpture Garden, Smithsonian Institution, Gift of Joseph H. Hirshhorn, 1966
Page 38

Bouquet of Concaves, 1959
Steel, painted
27 1/2 x 38 1/2 x 8 in.
The Phillips Collection, Washington, D.C., Gift of Gifford and Joann Phillips, 2008
Pages 83, 84 (detail), and cover (detail)

Bouquet of Concaves II, 1960
Steel, painted
22 x 21 3/4 x 9 in.
Private collection, courtesy McKee Gallery, New York
Pages 28 and 74

Black Concaves, 1960
Steel, painted
34 3/4 x 25 x 10 1/4 in.
The Honorable Ann W. Brown and Donald A. Brown
Pages 52, 53, and 77 (detail)

Paintings and Works on Paper

Untitled, 1950
Black and yellow egg ink and green ink on paper
15 1/2 x 20 1/4 in.
Baltimore Museum of Art, Gift of Edward Tuck, New York (BMA.1986.188)
Page 43

Untitled, c. 1951
Ink and tempera on paper
18 1/4 x 23 1/4 in.
Smithsonian American Art Museum, Museum purchase
Pages 32–33

Untitled, 1955
Clay
7 x 10 1/2 in.
Estate of David Smith, New York
Estate 808 PK
Page 43

Untitled, 1956
Oil and sand on canvas
73 1/8 x 11 in.
Hirshhorn Museum and Sculpture Garden, Smithsonian Institution, Museum Purchase, 1976
Page 85

Untitled, 1956
Oil on masonite
12 x 14 in.
Estate of David Smith, New York
Estate 7556.019
n.p. (detail); page 82

Untitled, 1956
Oil on canvas
12 5/8 x 14 13/16 in.
Estate of David Smith, New York
Estate 7556.013
Page 46

Untitled (Relief Painting), 1956
Plaster and oil on canvas, on wood
11 1/2 x 15 3/4 in.
Estate of David Smith, New York
Estate 8056.002
Pages 48–49

Untitled, 1957
Pencil, oil, and tempera on paper
20 1/3 x 26 1/8 in.
Estate of David Smith, New York
Estate 7357.059
Pages 58–59, 105 (detail)

Untitled, 1957
Egg tempera on paper
15 1/2 x 20 in.
Yale University Art Gallery, Charles B. Benenson, B.A. 1933, Collection
Page 37

Untitled, 1957
Spray enamel and oil on canvas
33 13/16 x 12 9/16 in.
Estate of David Smith, New York
Estate 7557.45
Page 47

First Ovals, 1958
Spray enamel on canvas
98 1/2 x 51 3/4 in.
Private collection,
courtesy Gagosian Gallery, New York
Estate 7558.002
Page 40

Untitled, 1958
Oil on canvas
83 1/4 x 26 in.
Estate of David Smith, New York
Estate 7558.018
Page 57

Untitled, 1958
Spray enamel on canvas
97 1/8 x 13 1/8 in.
Estate of David Smith, New York
Estate 7558.028
Page 17

Untitled (11-22-58), 1958
Brush and black ink and egg yolk
on laid paper
17 9/16 x 26 1/16 in.
National Gallery of Art, Washington, Gift of Candida and Rebecca Smith, in Honor of the 50th Anniversary of the National Gallery of Art, 1991.56.5
Page 44

White Egg with Pink, 1958
Oil and metallic paint on canvas
98 3/8 x 52 in.
Hirshhorn Museum and Sculpture Garden, Smithsonian Institution, Museum Purchase, 1977
Page 14

Night Window, 1959
Spray enamel on canvas
72 x 17 5/8 in.
Estate of David Smith, New York
Estate 7559.025
Page 51

Untitled, 1959
Black egg ink on paper
27 x 39 1/2 in.
The Phillips Collection, Washington, D.C., Gift of Linda Lichtenberg Kaplan, 2004
Page 81

Untitled, 1959
Spray enamel on canvas
98 x 51 in.
Estate of David Smith, New York
Estate 7559.020
Page 24

Untitled (9/3/59), 1959
Brush and black ink on wove paper
26 5/8 x 39 3/4 in.
National Gallery of Art, Washington, Gift of Candida and Rebecca Smith, in Honor of the 50th Anniversary of the National Gallery of Art, 1991.56.4
Page 30

Untitled, c. 1959
Spray enamel on canvas
38 1/8 x 32 in.
Private collection, Houston, courtesy of Waqas Wajahat, New York
Estate 7559.23
Page 18

Untitled, 1960
Egg ink and tempera on paper
24 x 38 in. (by sight)
Collection Joanna Shaw-Eagle
Page 21

Pushup of Concaves, c. 1961–63
Black egg ink on paper, in leather-bound sketchbook
10 1/2 x 8 1/2 in.
Estate of David Smith, New York
Estate Sketchbook 50
Page 61

Untitled, 1962
Enamel spray paint on wove paper
11 9/16 x 17 9/16 in.
National Gallery of Art, Washington, Gift of Candida and Rebecca Smith, in Honor of the 50th Anniversary of the National Gallery of Art, 1991.56.8
Pages 22–23

Untitled, 1962
Black, yellow, and gold spray enamel on paper
17 3/8 x 11 1/2 in.
Baltimore Museum of Art, Gift of the Board of Trustees and Staff in Honor of Suzanne F. Cohen, Chair (2003–2006); and purchase with exchange funds from Bequest of Saidie A. May (BMA.2006.45)
Page 3

Untitled, 1964
Spray enamel on canvas
14 7/8 x 31 1/2 in.
Estate of David Smith, New York
Estate 7564.308
Pages 21 and 108

Photographs

Suspended Figure, 1935, at Bolton Landing, c. 1936
Black and white photograph
Estate of David Smith, New York
Page 65

Oculus, 1947, with Lake George in background, c. 1947
Black and white print with cropping marks
Estate of David Smith, New York
Page 72

Self-portrait in the workshop at Bolton Landing, 1953
Black and white photograph
Estate of David Smith, New York
Pages 10–11

7/29/53, *Tanktotem III*, and *Tanktotem IV* photographed against Lake George, on the town dock at Bolton Landing, c. 1953
Black and white photograph
Estate of David Smith, New York
Page 67

Bicycle, *7/29/53*, *Tanktotem IV*, and *Tanktotem III* photographed against Lake George, on the town dock at Bolton Landing, c. 1953
Black and white photograph
Estate of David Smith, New York
Frontispiece and page 67

Tanktotem IV, 7/29/53, and *Tanktotem III* photographed against Lake George, on the town dock at Bolton Landing, c. 1953
Black and white photograph
Estate of David Smith, New York
Page 34

Tanktotem IV, 1953, at Bolton Landing, c. 1953
Black and white photograph
Estate of David Smith, New York
Page 25

Tanktotem V, 1955–56,
at Bolton Landing, c. 1956
Black and white photograph
Estate of David Smith, New York
Page 20

Tanktotem VI, 1957,
at Bolton Landing, c. 1958
Black and white photograph
Estate of David Smith, New York
Page 106

Bouquet of Concaves, 1959,
at Bolton Landing, 1959
Color slide transparency
Estate of David Smith, New York
Pages 29 and 71

Bouquet of Concaves, 1959,
at Bolton Landing, 1959
Black and white negative with cropping tape
Estate of David Smith, New York
Page 71

Bouquet of Concaves, 1959,
at Bolton Landing, 1959
Black and white photograph and annotations by David Smith,
Published in *Arts*, February 1960
Page 31

Works in progress on studio floor
at Bolton Landing, 1959
Black and white photograph with annotations by David Smith,
published in *Arts*, February 1960
Page 79 (detail)

Works in progress outside workshop
at Bolton Landing, 1959
Black and white photograph
Estate of David Smith, New York
Page 78

Bouquet of Concaves, 1959, and *August Raven*, 1960, in progress outside workshop at Bolton Landing, 1959
Black and white photograph
Estate of David Smith, New York
Page 47

Auburn Queen, 1959,
at Bolton Landing, c. 1959
Color slide transparency
Estate of David Smith, New York
Page 80

Circles and Angles, 1959,
at Bolton Landing, c. 1959
Color slide transparency
Estate of David Smith, New York
Page 39

Raven V, 1959, at Bolton Landing, c. 1959
Color slide transparency
Estate of David Smith, New York
Page 68

Sprays in the studio
at Bolton Landing, c. 1959–60
Black and white photograph
Estate of David Smith, New York
Page 26

Bouquet of Concaves II, 1960,
at Bolton Landing, 1960
Color slide transparency
Estate of David Smith, New York
Page 74

Tanktotem X and *Tanktotem VII*
at Bolton Landing, c. 1960
Black and white photograph
Estate of David Smith, New York
Page 50

Bolton Landing, 1961
Black and white photograph
Estate of David Smith, New York
Page 41

Zig I, 1961, at Bolton Landing
Black and white photograph
Estate of David Smith, New York
Page 56

Zig II, 1961, at Bolton Landing
Color transparency
Estate of David Smith, New York
Page 54

Zig II and *Zig III*, both 1961,
at Bolton Landing c. 1962–63
Black and white photograph
Estate of David Smith, New York
Page 55

Bec-Dida Day, 1963,
at Bolton Landing, c. 1963
Color slide transparency
Estate of David Smith, New York
Page 12

Self-portrait with *Zig III*
at Bolton Landing, c. 1963
Black and white negative with cropping marks
Estate of David Smith, New York
Pages 2 and 66

Zig III, 1961, at Bolton Landing c. 1963
Black and white photograph
Estate of David Smith, New York
Page 60

Zig III, 1961, and *Cubi XXIV*, 1964,
at Bolton Landing, c. 1964
Contact print
Estate of David Smith, New York
Page 73

Cubi XXVI, 1965, at Bolton Landing, 1965
Contact print with cropping marks
Estate of David Smith, New York
Page 107

Works not by David Smith

Dan Budnik (b. 1933)
Photographs of David Smith
at Bolton Landing, winter 1962–63
Pages 86–87, 94–95, 98–99, and 109 (detail)

Medardo Rosso (1858–1928)
Aetas aurea (Golden Age)
1886–87
Aristotype by the artist, experimental technique, enlarged detail, 12 x 8 cm, photo of a photo, cut in a corner and re-photographed; two marks left by fingerprints
Page 69 (bottom)

Constantin Brancusi (1876–1957)
View of the artist's studio, 1923,
published in *Minotaure*, 1933
Page 69

Henry Moore (1898–1986)
Reclining Figure, c. 1938
Photograph by the artist
Page 69

Photographic Credits

All photographs by Dan Budnik courtesy Dan Budnik. All photographs by David Smith courtesy Estate of David Smith.

Christie's, New York: pages 28, 74. CNAC/MNAM/Dist. Réunion des Musées Nationaux / Art Resource, NY: page 69 (center). Galerie Gmurzynska, Zürich: pages 48–49. Mitro Hood: page 43 (above). Jim Johnson Photography: page 21 (above). Gunther Knop Photography, New York, courtesy Pamela Auchincloss, New York: page 43 (below). Margo Leavin Gallery, Los Angeles: page 57. Robert McKeever, courtesy Gagosian Gallery: pages np, 17, 21(below), 36, 40, 46, 47 (above), 51, 58–59, 61, 82. Museo Medardo Rosso, Barzio, Italy; © Archivio Medardo Rosso 2010: page 69 (below). Henry Moore Foundation: page 69 (above). Images courtesy National Gallery of Art, Washington: 44, 30, 22–23. Greg Staley: pages 52, 83, 81. Lee Stalsworth: page 70. Jerry L. Thompson: page 42. Waqas Wajahat, New York: page 18.

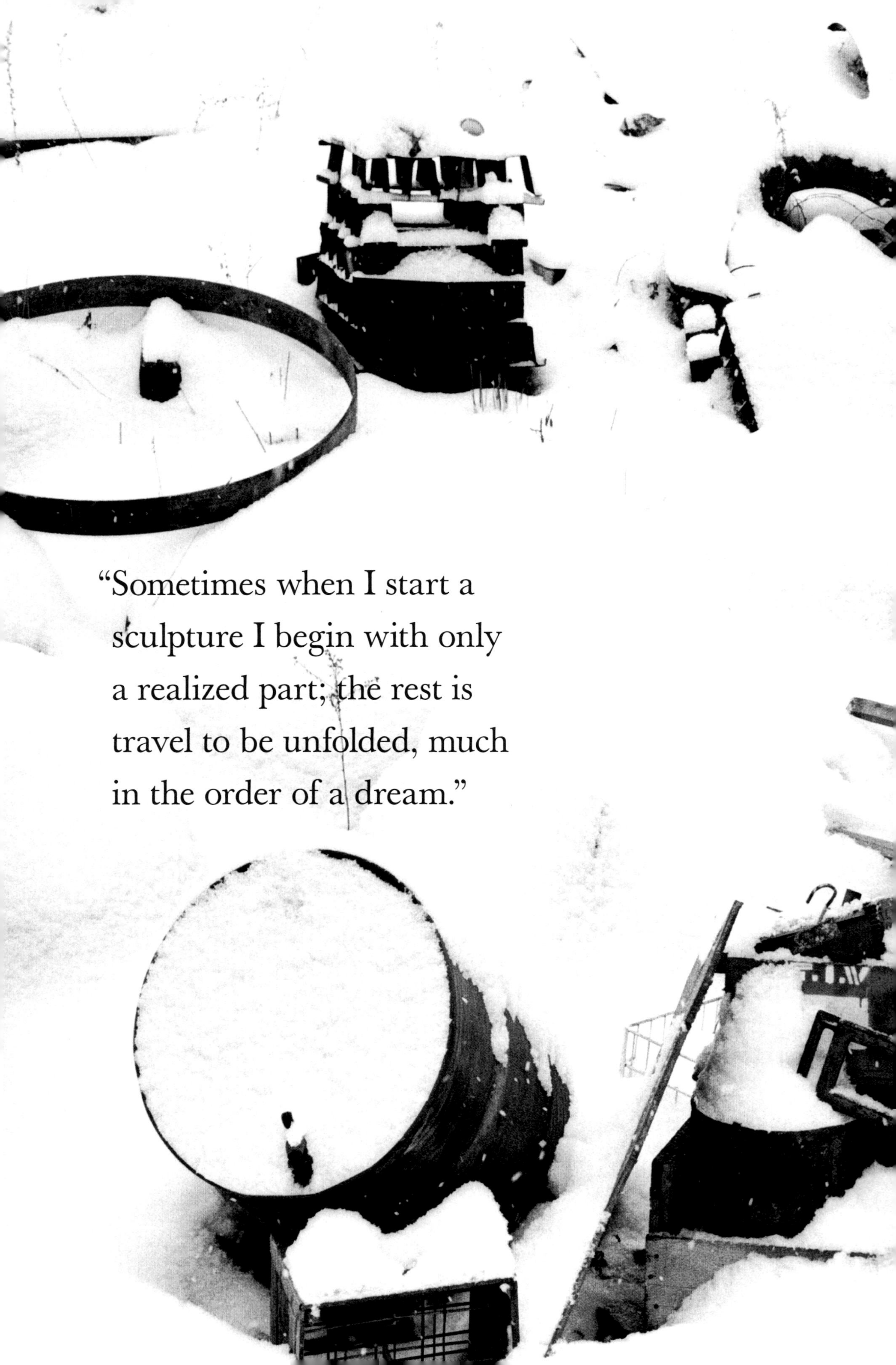

"Sometimes when I start a
sculpture I begin with only
a realized part; the rest is
travel to be unfolded, much
in the order of a dream."

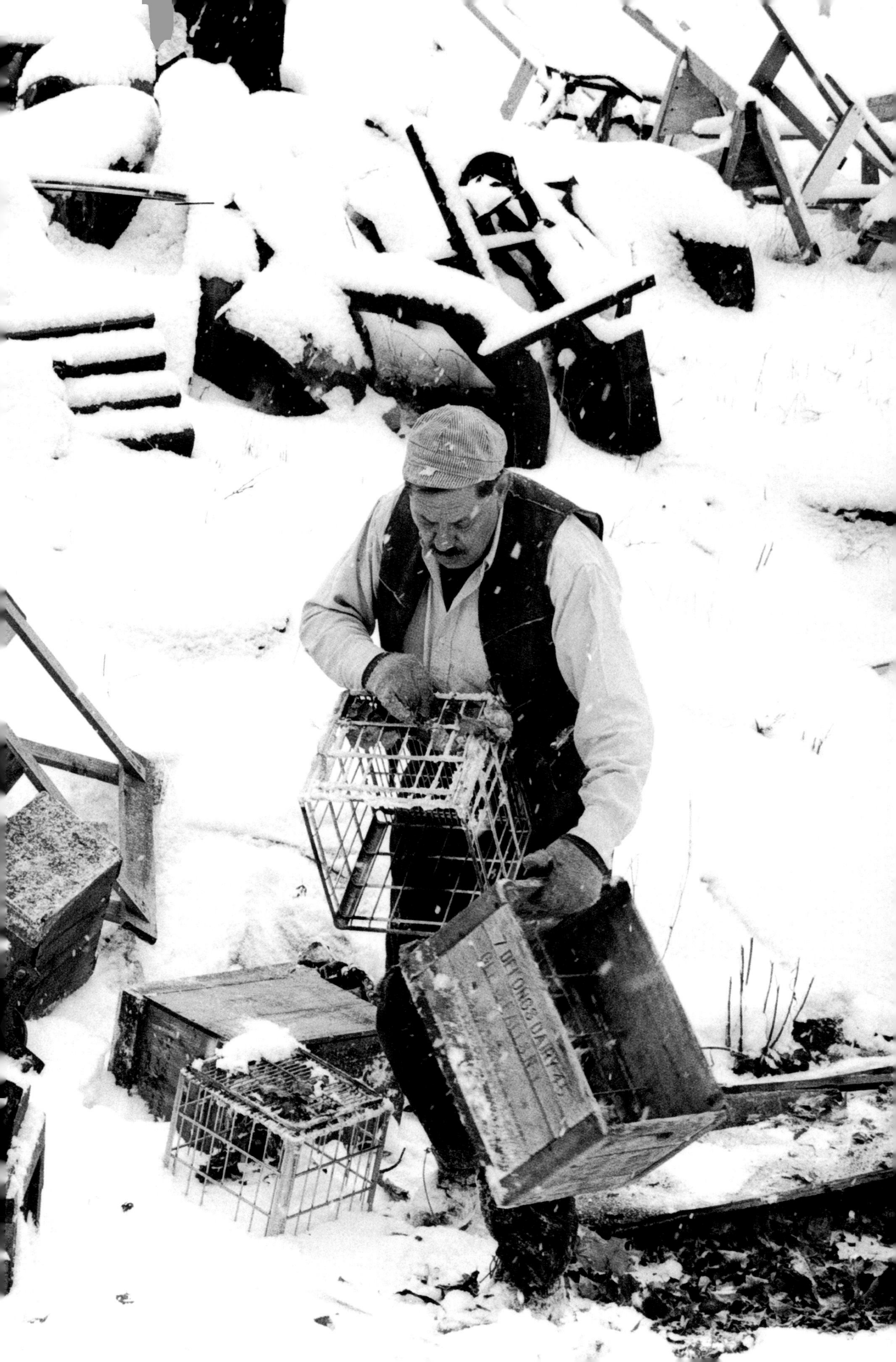

CHRONOLOGY

1906 Born David Roland Smith, March 9, 1906, in Decatur, Indiana.

1921 Family moves to Paulding, Ohio.

1924 Studies art at Ohio University, Athens (until 1925).

1925 Works during summer as welder and riveter for Studebaker automobile plant in South Bend, Indiana. Enters University of Notre Dame (fall); leaves after two weeks because there is no fine arts program. Returns to Studebaker (Finance Department).

1926 Moves to Washington, D.C., and then New York City; meets Dorothy Dehner. Takes evening classes at Art Students League.

1927 Full-time student at Art Students League until 1932; studies with John Sloan and Czech abstract painter Jan Matulka. In December, marries Dehner.

1928 Matulka introduces Smith to work of Wassily Kandinsky, Piet Mondrian, Pablo Picasso, and Russian constructivists.

1929 Visits friends at Bolton Landing (Lake George), New York; buys farm and spends summers working there until 1940, when he moves there permanently.

1930 Meets John Graham, who introduces him to Stuart Davis, Jean Xceron, Arshile Gorky, and Willem de Kooning. Sees photographs of welded metal sculpture by Picasso and Julio González in *Cahiers d'art*.

1931 Spends eight months in the Virgin Islands.

1932 Installs a forge and anvil at Bolton Landing; makes reliefs and constructions of wood, coral, wire, and plaster.

1933 Makes first welded iron sculptures. Exhibits paintings and drawings in group exhibition at Ferargil Galleries, New York.

1934 Establishes studio at Terminal Iron Works, a commercial shop on the waterfront in Brooklyn, New York.

1935 In October leaves with Dehner for Europe, with introductions from Graham to artists in Paris; visits Paris, Greece, Crete, Naples, Malta, Marseilles, Russia, and London.

1936 Returns to New York (July); makes first bronze works (reliefs).

1937 Joins the sculpture division of Works Progress Administration (WPA); works there until August 1939.

1938 First solo exhibition of sculpture and drawings at Marian Willard's East River Gallery, New York.

1939 Makes his first arc-welded sculptures.

1940 Moves permanently to Bolton Landing; renames his home and studio Terminal Iron Works. Employed as machinist in Glenn Falls, New York.

1941 Included in two traveling exhibitions organized by the Museum of Modern Art, New York.

1942 Moves to Schenectady and works the graveyard shift as a welder at the American Locomotive Company; commutes to Bolton Landing on weekends.

1943 The Museum of Modern Art purchases its first sculpture by Smith, *Head* (1938).

1944 Classified 4F by U.S. Army; quits job in Schenectady and moves back to Bolton Landing; begins working on sculpture full-time.

1945 Meets Jackson Pollock.

1948 Teaches at Sarah Lawrence College, New York (until 1950).

1949 Meets Jean Freas, student at Sarah Lawrence.

1950 Awarded John Simon Guggenheim Memorial Foundation Fellowship, which enables him to stop teaching, buy quality materials, and dramatically increase scale of his works. Meets Helen Frankenthaler. Asks Robert Motherwell to write an essay for his upcoming show at Willard Gallery. Dehner and Smith separate.

1951 Guggenheim Foundation Fellowship renewed. Exhibits at First São Paulo Bienal. Meets Kenneth Noland. Begins making sculpture in continuous series and related groups.

1952 Begins Tanktotems (1952–1960). Dehner and Smith divorce.

1953 Teaches at University of Arkansas, Fayetteville (spring). Marries Freas.

1954 Daughter, Rebecca, born (April 4). Included in XXVII Venice Biennale. Visits Europe as delegate to UNESCO's First International Congress of Plastic Arts (Venice); travels in France. Visiting Professor at Indiana University, Bloomington.

1955 Daughter, Candida, born (August 12). Teaches at the University of Mississippi, Oxford (fall).

1956 Begins to paint surfaces of his metal sculptures in expressionist style.

1957 The Museum of Modern Art organizes a major retrospective of Smith's work. Begins to work in stainless steel; makes first works on paper and canvas using commercial aerosol spray enamel.

1958 Represents the United States at the XXIX Venice Biennale. Smith and Freas separate.

1959 Awarded prize at V São Paulo Bienal. First major exhibition of his paintings, including the Sprays, is held at French and Company Gallery (September). Works with Hilton Kramer (editor of *Arts*) on "Special David Smith Issue." Begins creating small-scale, geometric, relief-like sculptures.

1960 Major solo sculpture exhibition at French and Company Gallery (February) includes forty-four works from 1956–60. *Arts* magazine publishes "Special David Smith Issue" (February).

1961 The Museum of Modern Art organizes traveling exhibition of fifty sculptures (1933–57). Begins the Zigs, his first large-scale, geometric, multi-level structures. Refuses third prize at Carnegie International for *Zig IV*. Begins Cubi series. Smith and Freas divorce.

1962 Invited to make two sculptures for the Fourth Festival of Two Worlds in Spoleto, Italy; produces twenty-seven sculptures in thirty days.

1963 Mark di Suvero and Anthony Caro visit Smith at Bolton Landing. Begins teaching at Bennington College, Vermont, once a week.

1964 Participates in Documenta III (Kassel, Germany). Awarded Creative Arts Award by Brandeis University, Waltham, Massachusetts.

1965 Appointed by President Lyndon B. Johnson to the National Council on the Arts (February). Dies May 23, in Bennington, Vermont, after his truck overturns.

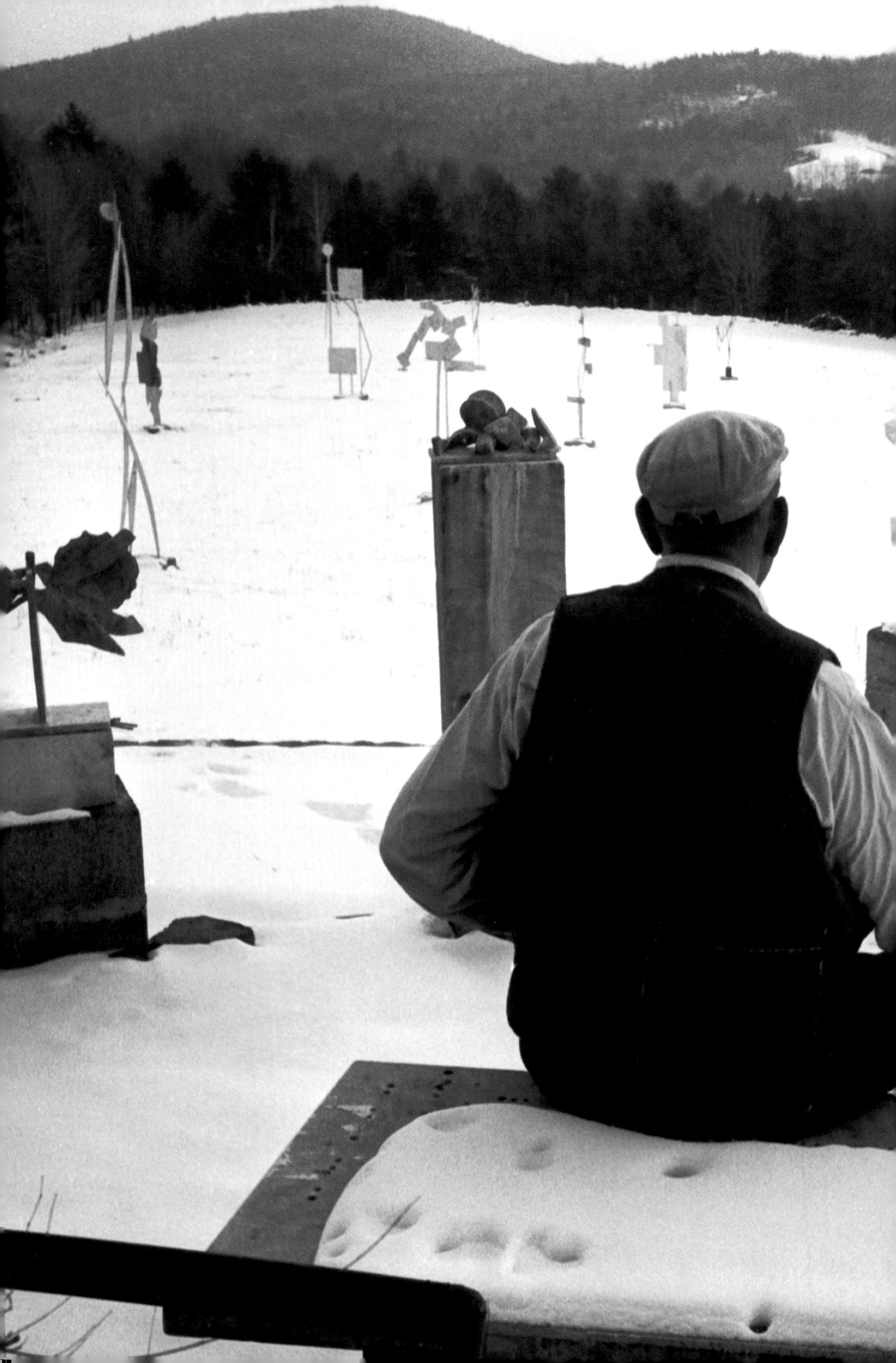

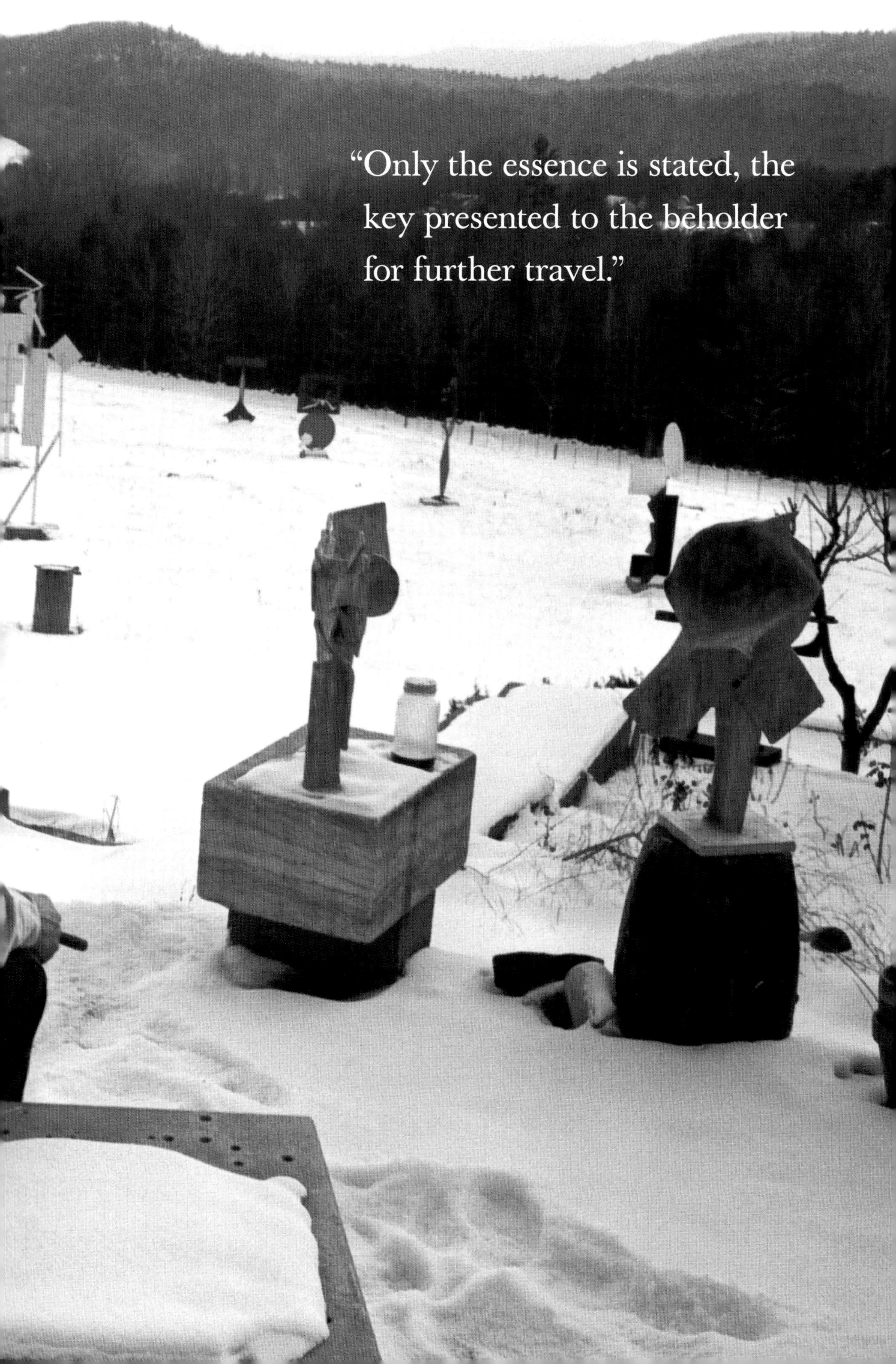

“Only the essence is stated, the key presented to the beholder for further travel.”

ACKNOWLEDGMENTS

The idea for an exhibition on David Smith began with his *Bouquet of Concaves* (1959), a sculpture given to The Phillips Collection in 2008. It quickly became apparent that this work held a significant place in Smith's imagination and was intimately connected to his activity as a draftsman and painter. *Bouquet of Concaves* became the catalyst for *David Smith Invents*, a fresh look at the moment when he shifted his focus from figurative sculpture to relief-like geometric assemblages, shortly before he began making monumental multipart structures.

Such a project can only be realized with the support and assistance of many people and institutions. I am deeply indebted to the Estate of David Smith for its ongoing support, generosity, and enthusiasm. The open access that the Estate has given me to its archives has been invaluable to the success of the project. Peter Stevens, executive director of the Estate, has generously offered insight and suggestions every step of the way. The detailed and thoughtful observations about *Bouquet of Concaves* that he expressed while visiting our conservation studio in summer 2008 provided a valuable framework for thinking about Smith's aesthetic vision. Susan Cooke, associate director of the Estate, has graciously shared her understanding of Smith with me and spent countless hours patiently fielding my questions and gathering images and other materials. I owe special thanks to Allyn Shepard at the Estate for her assistance.

The Phillips Collection is deeply indebted to kind and generous private collectors, including the Honorable Ann W. and Donald A. Brown, Joanna Shaw-Eagle, and others who wish to remain anonymous, who have given up their David Smith works for the period of this exhibition. David McKee deserves special gratitude for facilitating a key loan to the exhibition, making it possible to exhibit both versions of *Bouquet of Concaves* together, for the first time. We recognize the generosity of those public and private institutions that have lent works to the exhibition and contributed to its success: the Albright-Knox Art Gallery, Buffalo, N.Y., the Baltimore Museum of Art, the Hirshhorn Museum and Sculpture Garden, Smithsonian Institution, the National Gallery of Art, Washington, the Smithsonian American Art Museum, Storm King Art Center, Mountainville, N.Y., and Yale University Art Gallery, New Haven, Conn. In addition, without the assistance and support of the McKee Gallery in New York and Waqas Wajahat of New York, we would not have been able to secure certain private loans.

My thanks go to Larry Gagosian of the Gagosian Gallery in New York, for his generosity in providing photography and interim storage facilities for many of the Estate-owned works in the exhibition.

Many colleagues whom I met over the past two years have generously shared with me their ideas and insights about Smith, and several have also facilitated loans to the exhibition, including David R. Collens, Douglas Dreishpoon, Carol Eliel, Valerie Fletcher, David Getsy, Rena Hoisington, Albert Marshall, and Oliver Shell. Numerous people have contributed to the loan and publication process, and I would like to express my sincerest gratitude to them: L. Lynne Addison, Brianna Bedigian, Jennifer Belt, Suzanne Boorsch, Edward Bray, Dan Budnik, Kelly Carpenter, Mary Ann Carter, Monique Chardet, Amy Densford, Rebecca Endres, Alison Fenn, Jay Fisher, Ken Fleisher, Laura Fleischmann, Valerie Fletcher, Holly Frisbee, Suzanne Greenawait, Amanda Hamilton, Melissa Kroning, Lisa MacDougall, Arthur de Moras, Joann Moser, Elizabeth Reluga, Richard Sorensen, Aimee Soubier, John P. Stern, Kimberly Tishler, Keri Towler, Silvio Veronese, and Barbara C. G. Wood.

I want to express my sincere appreciation to Sarah Hamill, assistant professor at Oberlin College, for writing brilliantly about Smith's photographs. She has been the most generous of colleagues, sharing with me her expertise on Smith. The unknown photographs by him and others that she discovered during her research have been essential to the project. Special thanks are due to Kevin Sprouls of Skelton Design, who designed this book, and to Val Lewton, who designed the exhibition installation.

At The Phillips Collection, I want to thank all the colleagues who worked on this project in one fashion or another. The success of *David Smith Invents* is attributable to the many contributions made by museum staff, interns, and volunteers who shouldered so many responsibilities, especially, Sarah Anderson, Patricia Favero, Bill Koberg, Alec MacKaye, Stephanie Midon, Brooke Rosenblatt, Elizabeth Rice, Al and Sandra Schlactmeyer, Karen Schneider, Elizabeth Steele, Shelly Wischhusen, and Daniel Yett. I owe special thanks to Johanna Halford-MacLeod for her enthusiasm, dedication and advice, which have been vital to the success of the project. Above all, I thank my husband Clyde Frank for his patience and support.

Finally, I want to thank Dorothy Kosinski, director of The Phillips Collection, and Eliza Rathbone, chief curator, for their unfailing support and enthusiasm for this project from inception to realization.

Susan Behrends Frank
Associate Curator for Research
The Phillips Collection

Published on the occasion of the exhibition
David Smith Invents
organized by The Phillips Collection, Washington, D.C.

The Phillips Collection, Washington, D.C.
February 12–May 15, 2011

First published in the United States of America in 2011 by

The Phillips Collection
1600 21st Street, NW
Washington, D.C. 20009
www.phillipscollection.org

Published in association with

Yale University Press
P.O. Box 209040
302 Temple Street
New Haven, CT 06520-9040
www.yalebooks.com/art

Publication produced by
The Phillips Collection

Editor in Chief
Johanna Halford-MacLeod

Designer
Skelton Design

Printed in the United States of America

Cover: David Smith, *Bouquet of Concaves*, 1959, steel, painted (detail)

Frontispieces: Opposite page 1. David Smith, *Untitled*, 1956, oil on masonite (detail). Page 1. David Smith, *Tanktotem IV*, 1953, steel. Page 2. David Smith, Self-portrait with *Zig III* at Bolton Landing, c. 1963. Page 3. David Smith, *Untitled*, 1962, black, yellow, and gold spray enamel on paper. Page 4. David Smith's photograph of *Bicycle*, *7/29/53*, *Tanktotem IV*, and *Tanktotem III*, against Lake George, on the town dock at Bolton Landing, c. 1953.

End pages: Page 105. David Smith, *Untitled*, 1957, pencil, oil, and tempera on paper (detail). Page 106. *Tanktotem VI*, 1957, photographed by David Smith, c. 1958. Page 107. Contact print of *Cubi XXVI*, 1965, photographed by David Smith, 1965. Page 108. *Untitled*, 1964, spray enamel on canvas. Page 109. David Smith in the drawing studio at Bolton Landing, c. 1962–63, photograph by Dan Budnik (detail).

Library of Congress
Cataloging-in-Publication Data

Frank, Susan Behrends.

David Smith Invents / by Susan Behrends Frank.
p. cm.

Catalog prepared in conjunction with an exhibition held at the Phillips Collection, Washington, D.C., Feb. 12-May 15, 2011.

Summary: "Summary discusses selected steel sculptures fabricated by the American painter-sculptor David Smith (1906-1965), as well as Smith's drawings and paintings. Emphasizes his investigation of concave/convex forms, and notes his use of painted surfaces. Includes essays on Smith's photography of his own works and on his surfaces and materials" —Provided by publisher.

ISBN 978-0-300-16965-2 (alk. paper)

1. Smith, David, 1906-1965—Exhibitions.
2. Steel sculpture, American—Exhibitions.

I. Smith, David, 1906-1965.
II. Phillips Collection.
III. Title.

NB237.S567A4 2011

730.92—dc22

2010053145

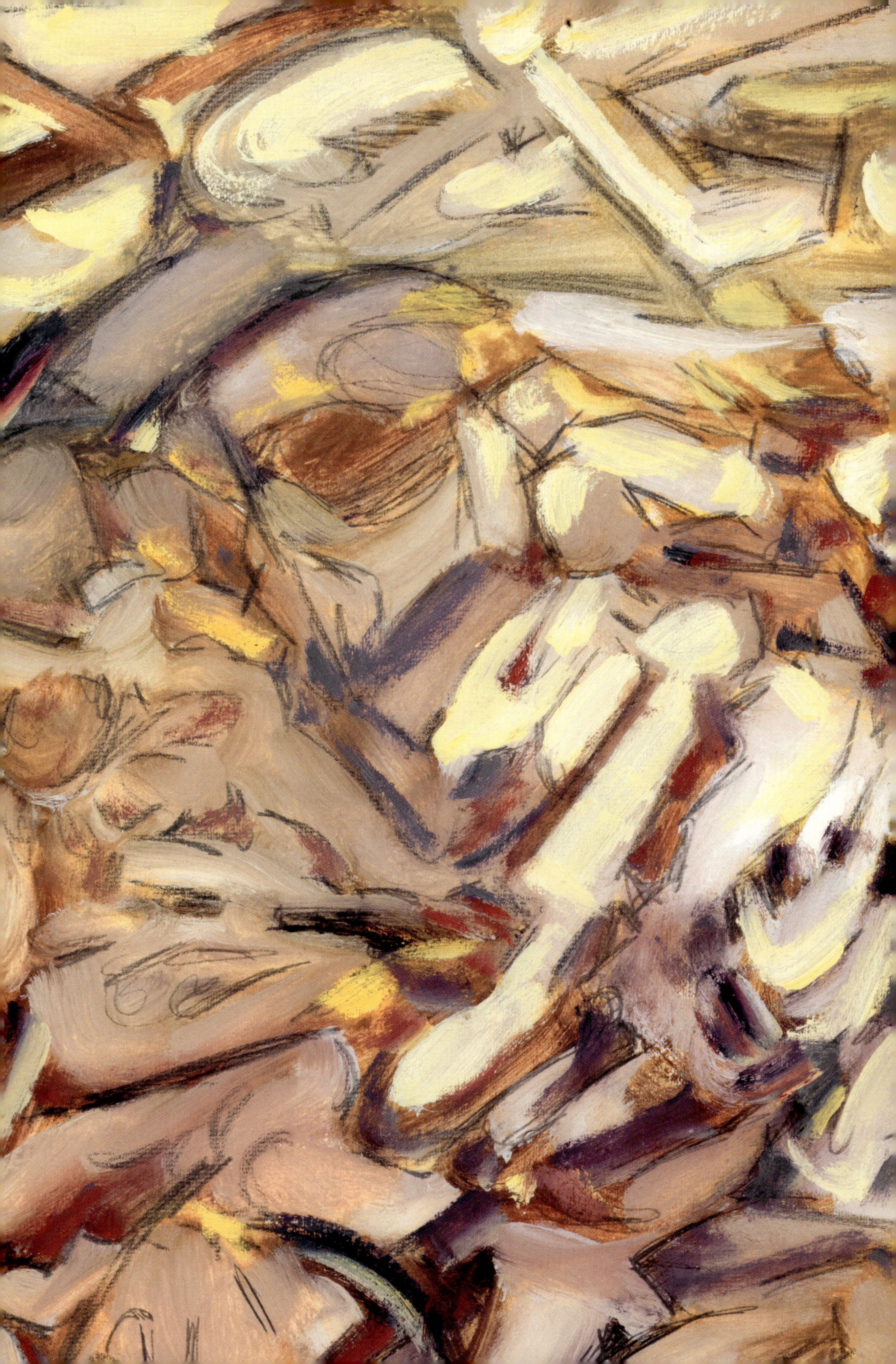

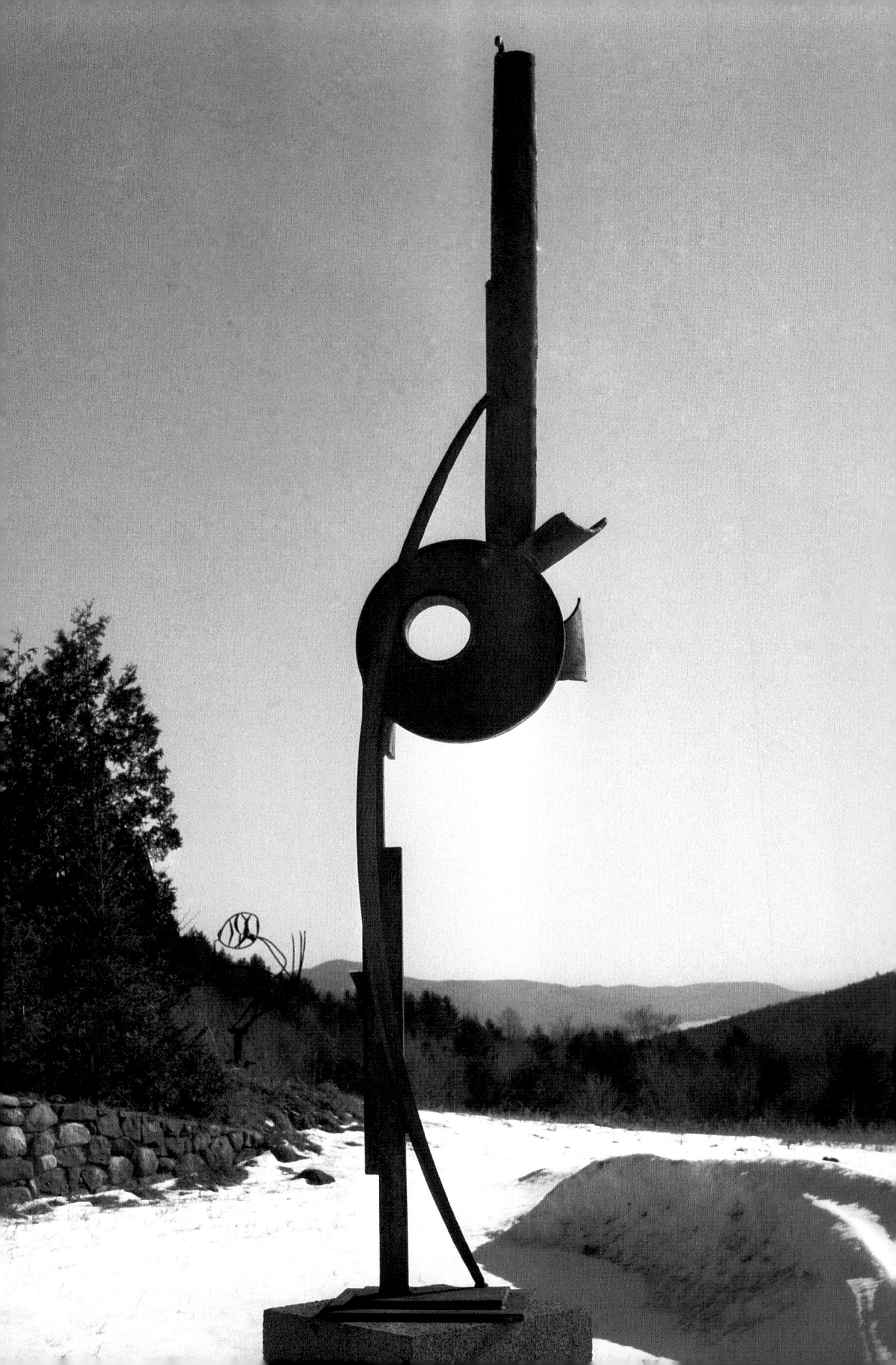

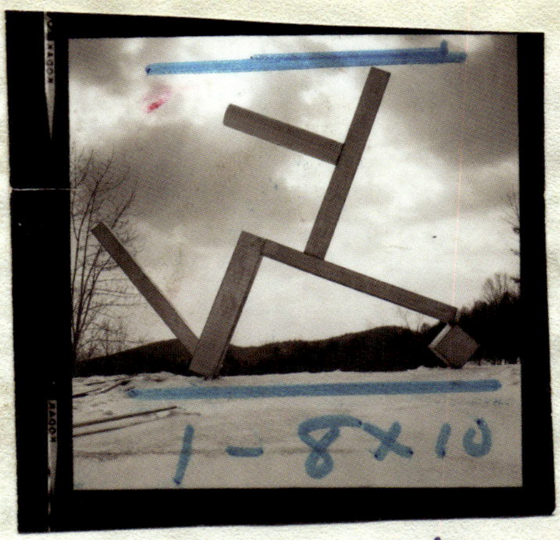

Cubi XXVI
'65

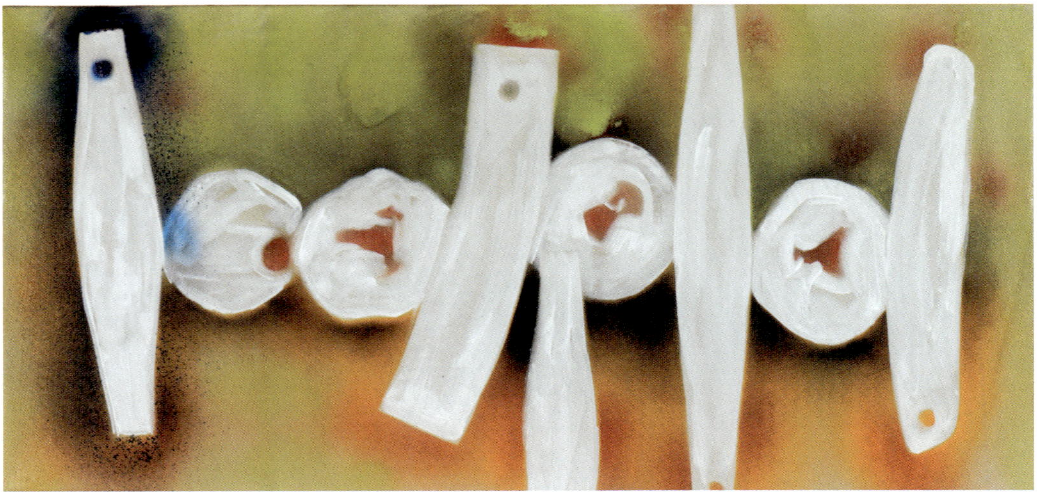

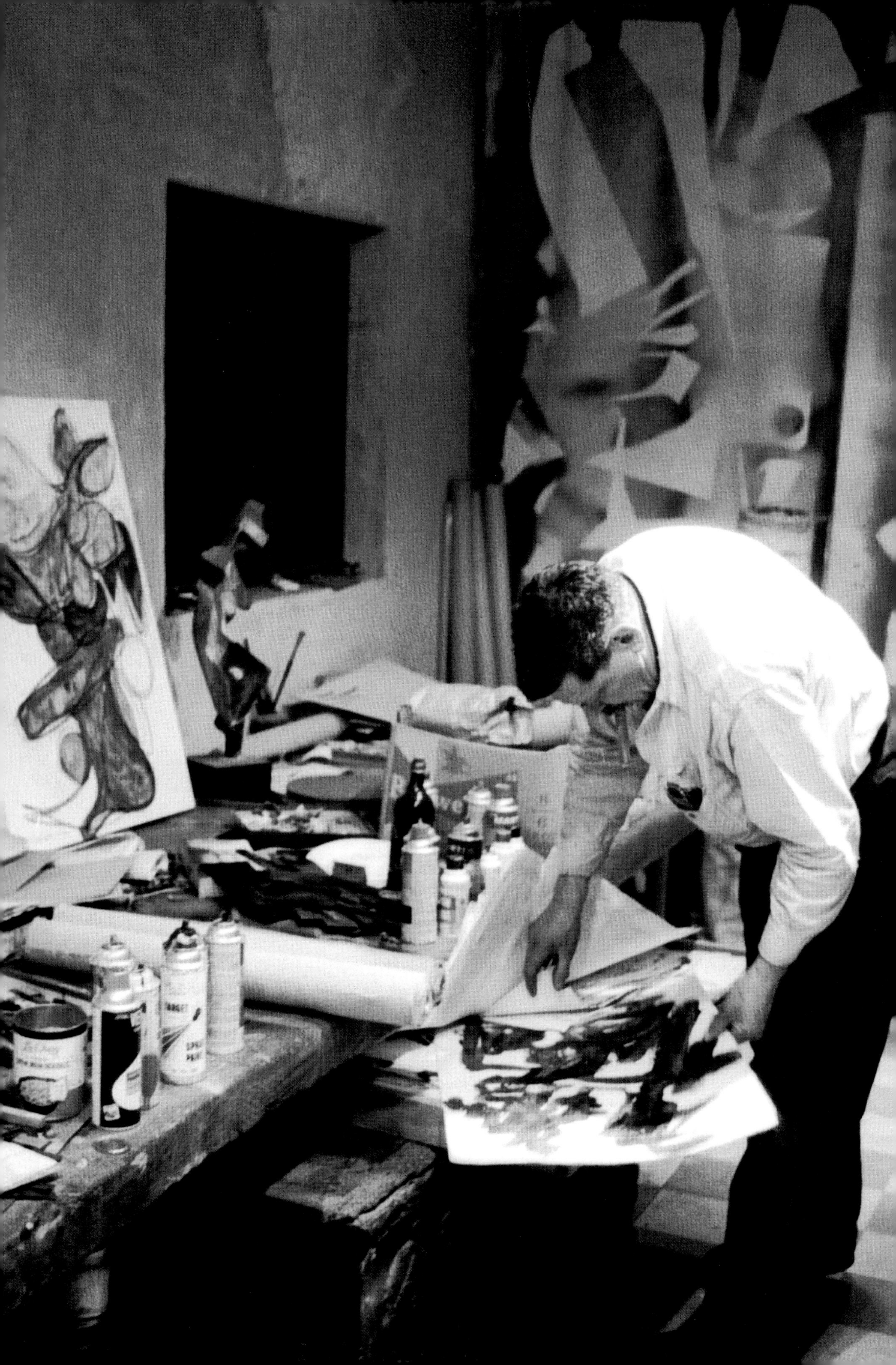